Key Concepts in
Early Childhood
Education and Care

The SAGE Key Concepts series provides students with accessible and authoritative knowledge of the essential topics in a variety of disciplines. Cross-referenced throughout, the format encourages critical evaluation through understanding. Written by experienced and respected academics, the books are indispensable study aids and guides to comprehension.

CATHY NUTBROWN
2ND EDITION

Key Concepts in
Early Childhood
Education and Care

Los Angeles | London | New Delhi
Singapore | Washington DC

SAGE Publications Ltd
1 Oliver's Yard
55 City Road
London EC1Y 1SP

SAGE Publications Inc.
2455 Teller Road
Thousand Oaks, California 91320

SAGE Publications India Pvt Ltd
B 1/I 1 Mohan Cooperative Industrial Area
Mathura Road
New Delhi 110 044

SAGE Publications Asia-Pacific Pte Ltd
33 Pekin Street #02-01
Far East Square
Singapore 048763

Library of Congress Control Number: 2010925341

British Library Cataloguing in Publication data

A catalogue record for this book is available from the
British Library

ISBN 978-1-84920-400-2
ISBN 978-1-84920-401-9 (pbk)

Typeset by C&M Digitals (P) Ltd, Chennai, India
Printed in Great Britain by CPI Antony Rowe, Chippenham Wiltshire
Printed on paper from sustainable resources

329815

contents

key concepts in early childhood
education and care

list of figures and tables

FIGURES

TABLES

acknowledgements

Students on the MA in Early Childhood Education at the University of Sheffield and many early years practitioners have suggested topics for inclusion in this second edition. I am grateful to them for their time and thoughtful comments. Particular thanks are due to Jacqui Lloyd, Michael Kubiak, Jools Page, Jackie Marsh and Frances Atherton and members of the Centre for the Study of Children, Families and Learning Communities, at the School of Education, University of Sheffield. Thanks, also, to all members of the publication team at Sage for their professional support throughout the development of this book.

Cathy Nutbrown
Sheffield
September 2010

The author and publisher would like to thank the following for permission to use figures material in the book:

Abbott L., Nutbrown C., *Experiencing Reggio Emilia*, (2001). Reproduced with the kind permission of Open University Press. All rights reserved.

Booth, T., Ainscow, M. and Kingston, D. (2006) *Index for Inclusion: developing play, learning and participation in early years and childcare.* Bristol, CSIE.

Cordes, C. and Miller, E. (eds) (2000) *Fool's Gold: A Critical Look at Computers in Childhood,* Alliance for Childhood www.allianceforchildhood.org.

Ministry of Education New Zealand (1996) *Te Whàriki* He Whàriki Màtaurangamò ngà Mokopuna o Aotearoa Early Childhood Curriculum Wellington New Zealand: Learning Media.

Moss, P. (2001) 'The Otherness of Reggio', in L. Abbott and C. Nutbrown (eds) *Experiencing Reggio Emilia: Implications for Preschool Provision.* Reproduced with the kind permission of Open University Press. All rights reserved.

NAEYC (2009) for the *12 principles of child development and learning* that has been excerpted and adapted from NAEYC's position statement 'Developmentally Appropriate Practice in Early Childhood Programs Serving Children from Birth through Age 8'.

The 12 principles are excerpted and adapted from NAEYC's position statement Developmentally Appropriate Practice in Early Childhood Programs Serving Children from Birth through Age 8. The full position statement is available by going online to: www.naeyc.org/positionstatements.dap. More information on the topic of developmentally appropriate practice is available at www.naeyc.org/DAP.

Two figures from *Research Studies in Early Childhood Education*, 2003. Trentham Books Ltd.

acknowledgements

ix

about the author

Cathy Nutbrown is Professor of Education and Director for Research at the School of Education, University of Sheffield. Cathy's work has involved the role of artists in residence in early years settings; Inclusion in the early years; children's rights; curriculum development; early literacy work with parents, and the ethical issues of research involving young children. Cathy teaches on the Masters and Doctoral Programmes in Early Childhood Education. Cathy began her career as a teacher of young children and has since worked in a range of settings and roles with children, parents, teachers, and other early childhood educators. Cathy is committed to finding ways of working 'with respect' with young children, and sees the concept of quality in the context of what it means to develop curriculum and pedagogy in the early years with the ambition of working in a climate of 'respectful education'. She is Editor in Chief of the *Journal of Early Childhood Research*. Her publications include: Nutbrown, C. (2011) *Threads of Thinking* (4th edn). London: Sage. She has authored several books with Sage and is author of over 30 journal papers.

introduction

This book aims to provide a series of starting points which will help readers to understand more about many key topics in early childhood education and care. In the rapidly changing field of early childhood education and care, it is becoming increasingly important for students and practitioners to have an awareness of many topics that relate to provision for young children. This book has five main aims:

- to provide starting points
- to describe key points
- to provide a clear focus on a range of issues
- to suggest connections between ideas, and
- to provide a confident beginning to study and understanding of important terms in early childhood education and care.

STARTING POINTS

Each entry is written to provide a starting point for understanding a key term. The entries are brief, covering basic points and principles and providing details of further reading for those who wish to take the study of any topic further.

KEY POINTS

In the space given to each entry it is not possible to provide comprehensive details of each topic featured in this book. The information contained in each is designed to provide an introduction to each and to highlight the key elements readers need to know in order to understand the concept under discussion. Suggestions for further reading which identify more detailed texts which deal in-depth with what is being discussed here are given at the end of each section.

FOCUS

This book introduces some 'key concepts' taken from numerous ideas, theories, practices and policies in the field of early childhood education and care. These 'concepts' are not *the* key concepts, but they are terms which most students and practitioners need some knowledge of. What is discussed here is not so much a 'map' of the territory of early childhood education and care but rather a 'travel brochure' for readers to decide what they want to explore further. The first edition was described by one reviewer as being like a box of chocolates – with plenty to choose from. To continue this metaphor, the topics featured in this second edition include some old favourites and some new; there are some 'soft centres' – favourite topics which people enjoy discussing and thinking about, and there are some 'hard nuts' – those more difficult issues which impact on the lives of some children and which it is important for all practitioners to know about.

The topics discussed in this second edition have been carefully selected by means of a survey of 500 early childhood education students and practitioners. Those chosen include a mixture of issues: types of practice, curriculum and assessment, philosophical underpinnings and some terms which have a place in the lore of early childhood education and care. Some terms which are of a narrow time frame determined by fleeting policies have not been included here because such information is better found on their dedicated web pages which are frequently updated.

CONNECTIONS

Each of the 'key concepts' detailed here is listed alphabetically in the contents list at the start of the book. As well as providing details of origins and definitions of each term, there is discussion of related research issues and examples of the term as applied in practice. Thus concrete examples make it possible to ground the discussion of each concept in the reality of practice.

A BEGINNING

Each entry in this book has been written to provide sufficient introductory information. This is not a dictionary or an encyclopaedia, but rather an introductory resource which provides confident beginnings to understanding the many terms which are central to working in and studying early childhood education and care. Further reading is listed at the end of each entry to assist readers in following up entries where they wish to know more. This book is a resource to point you in the right direction, a beginning.

assessment

> **Assessment is a part of the process of understanding what children know, understand and can do so that future teaching steps can be appropriately planned. It can involve observation, testing and discussion with children and/or their parents.**

Assessment of children's progress and learning is part of any educator's role and those who have worked with young children throughout the decades, (and centuries) have – in some way – assessed their learning and development. It is not possible to pinpoint when people first began to think about assessment in early education, but it is safe to say that famous pioneers of early education carried out assessments in order to understand what children were doing and thinking. Susan Isaacs, for example, used detailed observations of children's play to further her understanding of children's knowledge and understanding (Isaacs, 1929) and promoted views of children as capable and powerful learners, countering the deficit view of children's capabilities that was prevalent at the time.

Early assessment suffers from a problem of terminology. The word 'assessment' is currently in use in several contexts and carries many meanings of both purpose and practice. Because the same word is applied indiscriminately to three different purposes of assessment, there is an assumption that a shared understanding exists of what assessment means. This is far from the case and confusion over terminology continues throughout various policy developments in early years assessment. Nutbrown (2006) has suggested three different purposes for assessment in the early years, arguing that different tools are needed for different purposes: assessment for teaching and learning; assessment for management and accountability and assessment for research. *Assessment for teaching and learning* is defined as the process of identifying the details of children's knowledge, skills and understanding in order to build a detailed picture of the child's development and subsequent learning needs. *Assessment for management and accountability* prefers scores over narrative accounts of children's learning. Such assessments included the Baseline Assessment system which measured children's progress in predetermined objectives (SCAA, 1997) and allowed the 'value added' by the school to be calculated. *Assessment for research* includes those assessments (and often tests of 'scales' involving numerical outcomes) which are used specifically in research projects where quickly administered measures are needed and where uniformity of approach is necessary. One such example is the Sheffield Early Literacy Development Profile (Nutbrown, 1997) which was developed to measure aspects of early literacy of three to five year olds. Table 1 summarises the characteristics of each of these three purposes of assessment.

Assessment is an aspect of work in early childhood education which raises many research issues. Some key issues in research are:

- *Clarity of purpose* – is the reason for assessment of children clear?
- *Fitness for purpose* – is the assessment instrument or process appropriate for the reason that assessment is being carried out?
- *Authenticity* – do the assessment tasks appropriately reflect how children learn and what young children do?
- *Informed practitioners* – have adults who are assessing young children been appropriately trained and supported?
- *Child involvement* – how can children be fittingly involved in reflecting on their own learning and how can their views of their own learning and progress be incorporated into assessment for learning?
- *Respectful assessment* – what do practitioners understand by the notion of 'respect' in assessing children's learning and capabilities? Are assessments used in settings fair and honest with appropriate concern for children's well-being and involvement?
- *Parental involvement* – the roles of parents in the assessment of children's learning is under-researched. Their contribution to profiles of their children's learning and development is unique and more needs to be known about practices in this aspect of assessment.

Assessment of young children raises a number of concerns in relation to their well being and self-esteem. Roberts writes:

> Assessment and recording arrangements carry a world of hidden messages for children and parents. Is a positive model used, one which identifies

Table 1 Some characteristics of the three purposes of assessment

Assessment for teaching and learning	Assessment for management and accountability	Assessment for research
Focus on individuals	Focus on age cohort	Focus on samples
Concerned with details about each individual learner	Concerned with a sample of group performance	Concerned with performance of the sample
Is ongoing	Occurs within specific time frame	Takes place at planned points in a study
'Takes as long as it takes'	Is briefly administered or completed from previous assessment for teaching	Can be brief, depends on assessment and ages
Needs no numerical outcome to be meaningful	Numerical outcome provides meaning	Numerical outcomes often essential
Is open-ended	Often consists of closed list of items	Often consists of closed items
Informs next teaching steps	Informs management strategy and policy	Informs research decisions and findings – measures outcomes
Information relates primarily to individuals	Information relates primarily to classes, groups, settings or areas	Information relates to the sample, not to individuals or schools
Assessments required for each child	Some missing cases permissible	Some missing cases permissible
Main purpose is teaching	Main purpose is accountability	Purpose is to add to knowledge
Only useful if information is used to guide teaching	Only useful when compared to other outcomes (of other measures of cohorts)	Only useful as evidence of effectiveness of research study
Requires professional insight into children's learning	Requires competence in administration of the test	Requires competence in administration of the test
Depends on established relationship with individual children to be effective	Can draw on information derived through interaction with individual children, but not dependent on relationship	Often requires no previous relationship, but the ability to establish a rapport with the child at the time of the assessment
Requires ongoing professional development and experience	Requires short training session/learning the test and practice	Requires short training session/learning the test and practice

Source: Nutbrown, 2006: 128.

children's special strengths as well as areas for support? Is there accurate and detailed information about children? Do adults make sure that children share their successes, both with their parents and with each other?

These questions raise some of the issues which have a direct bearing on how children learn to see themselves. Attention to these sorts of details may have a profound effect on children's approach to learning. Our attention to them is surely the entitlement of every child. (Roberts, 1995: 115)

Observation is a crucial part of understanding and assessing children's learning. The following example demonstrates the importance of involving parents in assessing their children's learning.

> Sean was three and a half years old. He attended a nursery class each morning, where he spent much of his time playing outdoors, on bikes, in tents, climbing, gardening and running. His nursery teacher was concerned that he did not benefit from the other activities available indoors – painting, writing, drawing, construction, sharing books, jigsaws and so on. Even when some of these opportunities were placed outside, Sean still seemed to avoid them. The nursery teacher spoke with Sean's mother who said: 'We don't have a garden and there's nowhere for Sean to play outside – he hasn't got a bike and there's no park for climbing, or swings around here, or a space to do outside things, but we have lots of books and jigsaws, Lego, playpeople, we draw and make things. Sean was balancing his own curriculum but the adults involved needed to share what they knew in order to understand his learning needs and current capabilities. (Nutbrown, 1996: 49)

Practitioners continue to seek and develop practical ways of recording their observations of young children in order more fully to understand their play. The format in Figure 1 shows one way of linking observations and judgements about the meaning of those observations with plans for future teaching. Many similar formats for recording are used by practitioners.

REFERENCES AND INDICATIVE FURTHER READING

Clark, M. (2001) *Assessment in Early Childhood Settings: Learning Stories*. London: Paul Chapman Publishing.

DCSF (2008) *Statutory Framework for the Early Years Foundation Stage*. Nottingham: HMSO.

DfES/QCA (2003) *Foundation Stage Profile Handbook*. London: QCA.

NAME: Danika, Age 4			
Observation	**Analysis of Learning**	**Action**	**Date/ Initials**
Following a visit to some flats, D made a construction of cardboard boxes, piling one on top of the other – using a chair to reach.	Motor and symbolic representation of vertical schema. Work on 'higher' and 'lower'. Introducing vocabulary – using appropriate vocabulary	Move into counting boxes. Stabilising structure. More experiences of vertical, e.g. lifts and escalators.	
D on the climbing frame. Sliding down the slide. She said 'Going up'. Rolling cars and dolls down the slope.	Experimenting with forces and gravity	More experiences of slopes and rolling. Timing how long it takes to go down.	
D drew a picture. Lots of ///// lines. 'This is water falling out of the sky. It comes down and goes in the puddles' D said.	Understanding early scientific notions of rain and the environment	Maybe provide different kinds of pouring tools. Showerhead, watering can to encourage observation. Feed in appropriate language.	
D's mum reported that D is going to the top of the stairs and watching a ball bounce to the bottom; she's concerned.	Experiencing gravity and forces again	Need to provide acceptable safe experiences for observing, bouncing and dropping objects.	

Figure 1 *Example format for recording observation, analysis of learning and planned teaching action (Nutbrown, 2006)*

Drummond, M.J., Rouse, D. and Pugh, G. (eds) (1992) *Making Assessment Work*. London: NES Arnold/National Children's Bureau.

Isaacs, S. (1929) *The Nursery Years*. London: Routledge and Kegan Paul.

assessment

5

Nutbrown, C. (ed.) (1996) *Respectful Educators, Capable Learners: Children's Rights and Early Education*. London: Paul Chapman Publishing.

Nutbrown, C. (1997) *Recognising Early Literacy Development: Assessing Children's Achievements*. London: Paul Chapman Publishing.

Nutbrown, C. (2006) *Threads of Thinking: Young Children Learning and the Role of Early Education*, 3rd edn. London: Paul Chapman Publishing.

Roberts, R. (1995) *Self-esteem and Successful Early Learning*. London: Hodder & Stoughton.

SCAA (1997) *A National Framework for Baseline Assessment*. London: DfEE/SCAA.

Attachment Theory originally argued the importance of babies being in close relationship with their mother. Modern interpretation of attachment emphasises the importance of close, caring relationships between babies and their key carers.

Affection and Attachment are vital for young children's well-being ... Some practitioners may be anxious about assuming a parental role or even of taking some of the love properly due to the parent. It is safe to say that even very young babies will not confuse their carer with their parent and they are more likely to suffer from the lack of a close personal relationship at nursery. (Gillespie Edwards, 2002: 22)

The part adults play is key to young children's healthy development Positive and close relationships with adults are crucial for *all* children, including those away from their own homes and parents during the day. As Gammage argues:

The early nurturance of very young children and the importance of consistent high-quality attachment between the caregiver and the child are in themselves recognized as *the* vital components in optimal brain development; a part of every child's birthright and pivotal features in carefully crafted loving, educational and socio-emotional experience from birth. These are essential ingredients if the brain is to achieve something akin to its real potential, and if humans are to grow into fully functioning, creative and caring adults. (Gammage, 2006: 235, original emphasis)

Originally, and continually controversial, Bowlby's (1953, 1969) Attachment Theory spotlighted the need, in particular, for young children to be in the care of warm responsive adults (initially it was thought that mothers were the only person who could provide this). However, Vorria et al. (2003) found that children's capacity for attachment was related to the children's cognitive and psychosocial development, their behaviour, temperament and the sensitivity of their caregivers. Rutter (1972: 25) suggests that infants can form multiple attachments concluding that: 'If the mothering is of high quality and is provided by figures who remain the same during the child's early life, then (at least up to four or five mother figures) multiple mothering need have no adverse affects.'

Rutter's view was that, provided the multiple relationships made with the child were stable and good childcare was provided, the child was unlikely to suffer if they were not constantly with their mother. Indeed, some may argue that a *lack* of multiple attachments in the early part of life could also be detrimental to babies' social development!

Attachment Theory has had a troubled past and been used and manipulated throughout its history for economic and political ends. Bowlby's theory that children attach themselves to one main figure has long been debated – variously used as a 'stick' to beat working mothers, as a politically expedient tool, in relation to the economy, the workforce and as a rationale for flexible working hours, and so on. Bowlby's study became the object of political debate and was used by post-war pressure groups to argue that women should stay at home to rear their young.

Attachment and relationships between babies and their caregivers continues to be a focus of interest to researchers (Lee, 2006). The day-care context, Lee suggests, can have a significant impact on the development of close and supportive relationships between carer and child. Lee concluded:

> Building a firm relationship between infant and caregiver was a mutually beneficial and meaningful experience for both the infant and the caregiver. Relationship development also made for easy and smooth communication, sharing of thoughts and emotions, and mutual understanding between infant and caregiver. In addition, the infants and the caregivers made an effort to fine tune their behaviours in response to each other's development and change continuously, which is crucial in maintaining a firm relationship. (Lee, 2006: 146)

The implications of Bowlby's controversial theory have been argued and debated for over half a century since and contributed to the ongoing controversy about day care for children with critics of Attachment Theory claiming that secure attachment is not always necessary for healthy development and arguing (Hennessy et al., 1992). The Effective

Provision of Pre-School Education project (EPPE) concluded that: 'The quality of the interactions between children and staff were particularly important; where staff showed warmth and were responsive to the individual needs of children, children made more progress' (Sylva et al., 2004: 3).

Attachment is at the core of the 'key person approach' (Elfer et al., 2003) which places high importance on close and specific relationships between practitioners, children and parents.

REFERENCES AND INDICATIVE FURTHER READING

Bowlby, J. (1953) *Child Care and the Growth of Love*. Baltimore, MD and London: Pelican/Penguin.

Bowlby, J. (1969) *Attachment and Loss: Vol. 1. Attachment*. New York: Basic Books.

Elfer, P., Goldschmied, E. and Selleck, D. (2003) *Key Persons in the Nursery: Building Relationships for Quality Provision*. London: David Fulton.

Gammage, P. (2006) 'Early childhood education and care: politics, policies and possibilities', *Early Years*, 26(3): 235–48.

Gillespie Edwards, A. (2002) *Relationships and Learning: Caring for Children from Birth to Three*. London: National Children's Bureau.

Hennessy, E., Martin, S., Moss, P. and Melhuish, E. (1992) *Children and Day Care: Lessons from Research*. London: Paul Chapman Publishing.

Lee, S.Y. (2006) 'A journey to a close, secure and synchronous relationship: infant–caregiver relationship development in a childcare context', *Journal of Early Childhood Research*, 4(2): 133–51.

Rutter, M. (1972) *Maternal Deprivation Reassessed*. London: Penguin.

Sylva, K., Melhuish, E.C., Sammons, P., Siraj-Blatchford, I. and Taggart, B. (2004) *The Effective Provision of Pre-School Education (EPPE) Project: Technical Paper 12 – The Final Report: Effective Pre-School Education*. London: DfES/Institute of Education, University of London.

Vorria, P., Papaligoura, Z., Dunn, J., van IJzendoorn, M.H., Steele, H., Kontopoulou, A. and Sarafidou, Y. (2003) 'Early experiences and attachment relationships of Greek infants raised in residential group care', *Journal of Child Psychology and Psychiatry*, 44(8): 1208–20.

attachment

babies' learning and development

With changes in legislation and increased provision for babies and young children under three, ways of working with children in their first three years have received more attention. For the purposes of early childhood education and care, babies are the youngest children, aged from birth to the point where they begin toddling.

The years from birth to three are now receiving more interest and attention from policy-makers, as provision increases and as practitioners learn more about what the youngest children need for healthy, holistic development in their earliest years. Since the mid-1990s more interest has been shown in the professional development of those working with babies and toddlers (Goldschmied and Selleck, 1996; NCB/BBC, 1995; OPU/MMU, 2000). Government interest in the quality of provision for the youngest children led to the widely disseminated Birth to Three Matters Framework (DfES, 2002). It was published to promote effective practice in working with children in the first three years of life and its launch included nationwide training events. The Framework was designed as a source of support, information and guidance for those working with babies, toddlers and young children under three years of age. The Framework clearly stated that it:

- values and celebrates babies and children;
- recognises their individuality, efforts and achievements;
- recognises that all children have, from birth, a need to develop, learning through interaction with people and exploration of the world around them. For some children, this development may be at risk because of difficulties with communication and interaction, cognition and learning, behavioural, emotional and social development or sensory and physical development;
- recognises the 'holistic' nature of development and learning;
- acknowledges, values and supports the adults that work with babies and young children;

key concepts in early childhood education and care

- provides opportunities for reflection on practice;
- informs and develops practice whilst acknowledging that working with babies and young children is a complex, challenging and demanding task and that often there are no easy answers (DfES, 2002: 4).

From 2008, the distinct phase for babies and toddlers was subsumed into a new framework designed to encompass the years from birth to five, this raised some fears that the youngest children may be marginalised in favour of attention given to children in the later stage of the age range (the three to five year olds). Only time will tell.

In Scotland (Learning and Teaching Scotland, 2005) the policy document on under threes, *Birth to Three: Supporting our Youngest Children*, uses different terms and expressions to describe and discuss the particular nature of work with under-threes. The Scottish policy is built on three, clearly interrelated, *key features of effective practice* in work with children from birth to three:

- relationships;
- responsive care;
- respect.

Within this rubric are *five shared principles* which are intended to apply, whatever the setting or service providing for the youngest children. They are:

- the best interests of children;
- the central importance of relationships;
- the need for all children to feel included;
- an understanding of the ways in which children learn;
- equality, inclusion and diversity.

In their book, *The Scientist in the Crib: Minds, Brains and How Children Learn*, Gopnik et al. (1999b) draw on theories of cognitive and developmental psychology to demonstrate the capacities of young babies and toddlers to learn and illustrate the complexity of their learning abilities. Developmental psychology has provided some evidence to help us to understand why some elements of practice have always been enjoyed by babies; for example, Gopnik and Schulz (2004) have shown how infants and young children have the prerequisites for making causal inferences particularly in their ability to learn from imitation. Babies can understand and imitate some quite complex actions of others (Meltzoff and Prinz, 2002) this is how they begin to learn social behaviour.

Studies in neuroscience (Greenfield, 1997; Greenough, 1987), the scientific study of the nervous system, have shed new light on how the brain develops and so led to the rethinking of some long-accepted beliefs about what babies could and could not do. Psychiatrist and neuroscientist Eric Kandel argued that the purpose of neuroscience was to help us to understand what happens in the brain. He wrote:

> The task of neural science is to explain behaviour in terms of the activities of the brain. How does the brain marshal its millions of individual nerve cells to produce behaviour, and how are these cells influenced by the environment … ? The last frontier of the biological sciences – their ultimate challenge – is to understand the biological basis of consciousness and the mental processes by which we perceive, act, learn, and remember. (Kandel et al., 2000: 7)

It is not necessary for early years practitioners to understand the physiology of the brain, or to be fully conversant with the development and functioning of the nervous system. The detail of the complex field of neuroscience and neuropsychology gives us a confidence to trust what we see in babies, and to trust that the complex and rapid development which takes place in the first year of life is fuelled by nature and supported and extended by the environments and relationships in which children are nurtured.

Neuroscience endorses what many practitioners and parents have long known, such as the fact that young babies can distinguish one human face from another, and that even quite young babies can recognise a familiar face (Gopnik et al., 1999a). We now *know* that babies can get bored and need interesting surroundings, company and stimulation, yet parents and carers knew this long before any study provided the 'proof'. As Brierley noted: 'The brain thrives on variety and stimulation. Monotony of surroundings, toys that only do one thing are soon disregarded by the brain' (1994: 82).

Even newborn babies can show preferences for certain objects and images (Gopnik et al., 1999a) and babies can differentiate between objects to seek out. Evidence from scientific research does, however, provide useful information to those working with the youngest children who no longer need to rely solely on instinct and personal observation. Studies now suggest, as many parents of new babies have known, that babies quickly recognise familiar faces, and though they may not call this process of human recognition 'habituation' (Gopnik et al., 1999a: 27) they know that their babies know them!

Other similar studies (Meltzoff and Moore, 1999; Gammage, 2006) have further developed current knowledge of the levels of understanding that babies and young children develop throughout the first three years of their life. Research suggests that babies are born with innate tendencies of curiosity and recognition, and so adults can confidently harness these natural tendencies in order to support those early skills. Through the provision of appropriate stimulating environments which interest babies and nurture their learning and development, practitioners are building on babies' inbuilt desire to discover. Staff in infant/toddler rooms must make room in their very busy days to focus on each child, offering him or her the opportunity to experience the warmth and enjoyment of child-centred and responsive shared reading sessions (Makin et al., 2006: 275).

Wailling (2005) identified three high-frequency triggers: noise, movement and being outdoors. She writes:

> *Noise*, ranging from an adult calling the baby's name to an unexpected clash of toys, immediately resulted in visual attention being given ... *Movement –* ranging from that of a pop up toy to that of passing people – also attracted the babies' attention ... Movement triggered scanning and tracking responses in the babies as well as their sustained attention ... When *out of doors* the babies scanned and tracked their immediate horizons and once fixed on an object of interest, passing children, the black edge of the buggy rain cover, the movement of the garden shrub when being placed on the ground in the car seat before being strapped into the car, appeared almost hypnotised by the imagery. (p 52)

Trevarthen (1977), inspired by the work of Bruner, writes: 'I became convinced that an exceedingly complex innate mechanism foreshadowing the co-operative intelligence of adults and more general than the mechanism of language, was already functioning in early infancy' (Trevarthen, 1977: 7). Some educationalists regard Trevarthen's work as evidence to support growing assertions that babies can think and that their environments for learning should be tailored to support such thinking.

The effectiveness of the English national policy framework for practice with babies has still to be evaluated and the ways in which practitioners in home and group settings initiatives various policy documents and initiatives needs still to be understood. However, the principles which underpin the elements of the Early Years Foundation Stage which apply to babies are only effective if they are fundamentally based on respectful attention to what young children can do and what they need for healthy holistic growth and development. The importance of the United Nations Convention on the Rights of the Child and the role of practitioners working with the youngest children is clear. There is much space for research in this work. However, the ways in which the policy frameworks for the care and development of babies are realised in practice will be of great interest. Most important, perhaps, will be the development of a bank of case studies which tell real-life stories of babies, toddlers and practitioners in collaboration with parents to demonstrate how young children are supported in their growth, learning and development in their earliest years. With increased interest in neuroscience and the capacity of babies to communicate and form early relationships with other babies, there is a need for studies which help parents, policy-makers and practitioners to make decisions about how best to support their early years of learning.

The following example demonstrating sensitive approaches towards relationships is taken from Scotland's guidance on working with children under three.

Calum, 16 weeks old, is a new arrival at nursery. He is settling well and his Key Person, Heather, is able to tell Calum's parents that he is content throughout the day. Calum's mother, however, is distressed each morning as she leaves Calum and tells Heather that she is concerned that Calum is upset during the day and that the nursery is not telling her. Calum's mother has taken to phoning the nursery several times each day from work, asking to speak to Heather. This is not always possible, as Heather is busy and occupied with the children. This is making Calum's mother increasingly concerned. The nursery manager explains to Calum's mother that Heather is busy with the children and offers to check on Calum herself each day and report back, but Calum's mother prefers to hear directly about Calum's day from Heather.

Heather and the other three members of staff in the baby room, all of whom are building relationships with both Calum and his parents, discuss the situation with the nursery manager and share their views on how well Calum is settling and how best to reassure Calum's mother. Staff members agree that while Calum has settled very well, his mother needs to be reassured of this and needs to feel more included in his day. They decide, with the permission of Calum's parents, to take the opportunity to use the video camera to take footage of Calum at different points each day to give to his mother to take home with her, in addition to the digital photographs on display, so that she is able to see that he is contented and settling well. (Learning and Teaching Scotland, 2005: 16)

Nutbrown and Page (2008) suggest that high-quality planned experiences for children can best be provided by skilled and knowledgeable adults who know and understand the children's interests, and with whom the children have secure and trusting relationships. The Key Person is ideally placed to carry out this role as she or he will be attuned to the individual behaviour of the children and to be a facilitator for their patterns of play.

Heidi had set out the room for a Heuristic play session. The children arrived and started their explorations. Eighteen month old twin boys Barney and Will like to be close to one another. They share the same Key Person but have quite distinct and different personalities. Barney is shy and likes to take his time to check things out before attempting to explore. Will has a tendency to have a go at anything and nosily explores his environment. Will picks up one of the large tins and puts his face into it and shouts. He can hear his voice and he repeats the action. Barney stays close to Heidi who is sitting in a low chair. Heidi gestures to Barney as he picks up a large pebble and drops it into another tin. It crashes to the bottom. Will stops what he is doing and looks up as he hears the loud sound of the pebble crashing into the tin. Will toddles over to the tin and drops in another pebble but Barney winces at the sound. Instead he sits close to Heidi and explores the bottle tops and chains that lie piled upon one another. Barney picks up the largest chain and gently lets it slip through his fingers. It drops to the floor, the fluidity and weight of the chain results in it recoiling itself into another pile. Barney continues with his exploration, this time using a piece of rope. He holds the rope in one hand and the chain in the other and raises his hands up and down in turn, first the rope and then the chain. He lets them drop to the floor and then picks them up again. He repeats this action over and over. Heidi counts him doing this fifteen times. Meanwhile Will has found a selection of stones and is busy dropping them into any turned-up receptacle he can find, laughing gleefully as each stone drops to the bottom. He waits to hear the sound the stone makes at the bottom of each container. He drops a stone into a tube with no bottom in it and, hearing no sound investigates further. He puts his arm into the tube and as he reaches the bottom realises he can touch the carpet. With the tube still attached Will lifts his arm and starts to giggle. Heidi smiles at him and gently removes the tube as she sees that Will is about to become a little distressed because he is unable to shake it off. Barney looks up at Heidi as she smiles warmly affirming his attempt to investigate the chains and rope. Some time later when the children were clearly coming to the end of their play, Heidi begins to involve the children in clearing up the room. The children know what they have to do and immediately start to help to fill the drawstring bags with the things on the floor. The tidying complete, Will rushes to the door ready to go out, Barney hangs back and holds his arms up to Heidi. She offers her hands to the boys as they rejoin the rest of the nursery. (Nutbrown and Page, 2008: 16)

REFERENCES AND INDICATIVE FURTHER READING

Abbott, L. and Langston, A. (2005) *Birth to Three Matters: supporting the Framework of Effective Practice*. Buckingham: Open University Press.

Breirley, J. (1994) *Give Me a Child Until He Is Seven: Brain Studies and Early Childhood Education*, 2nd edn. London: Falmer Press.

David, T., Goouch, K., Powell, S. and Abbott, L. (2002) *Review of the Literature: Birth to Three Matters: A Framework to Support Children in their Earliest Years*. London: Department of Education and Skills/Sure Start.

DfES (2001) *National Standards for Under Eights Day Care and Childminding*. London: DfES Publications.

DfES (2002) *Birth to Three Matters: An Introduction to the Framework*. London: DfES Publications. Also available at: wwws/surestart.gov.uk

DfES/QCA (2000) *Curriculum Guidance for the Foundation Stage*. London: DfES Publications.

Gammage, P. (2006)'Early childhood education and care: politics, policies and possibilities', *Early Years*, 26, (3) 235–48.

Goldschmied, E. and Selleck, D. (1996) *Communication between Babies in their First Years*. London: National Children's Bureau.

Gopnik, A., Meltzoff, A. and Kuhl, P. (1999a) *How Babies Think*. London: Weidenfeld & Nicholson.

Gopnik, A., Meltzoff, A. and Kuhl, P. (1999b) *The Scientist in the Crib: Minds, Brains and How Children Learn*. New York: William Morrow.

Gopnik , A. and Schulz, L. (2004) *Mechanisms of Theory-formation in Young Children*.

Greenough, W.T., Black, J.E and Wallace, C. S. (1987) 'Experience and brain development', *Child Development*, 58: 569–82.

Greenfield, S. (1997) *The Human Brain*. London: Weidenfeld & Nicholson.

Kandel, E.R., Schwartz, J.H. and Jessell, T.M. (2000) *Principles of Neural Science*, 4th edn. New York: McGraw-Hill.

Learning and Teaching Scotland (2005) *Birth to Three: Supporting our Youngest Children*. Edinburgh: Learning and Teaching Scotland.

Makin, L., Jones Daiz, C. and McLachlan, C. (2006) *Literacies in Childhood: Changing Views, Challenging Practice*. NSW: Elsevier.

Manning-Morton, J. and Thorp, M. (2001) *Key Times – a Framework for Developing High Quality Provision for Children Under Three*. London: Camden Under Threes Development Group and the University of London.

Meltzoff, A.N. and Moore, M.K. (1999) 'A new foundation for cognitive development in infancy: the birth of the representational infant', in E.K. Scholnick, K. Nelson, S. Gelman and P.H. Miller (eds) *Conceptual Development: Paiget's Legacy*. Mahwah, NJ: Erlbaum Press.

Meltzoff, A.N. and Prinz, W. (2002) *The Imitative Mind: Development, Evolution and Brain Bases*. Cambridge: Cambridge University Press.

NCB/BBC (1995) *Tuning In to Children*. London: NCB/BBC.

Nutbrown, C. and Page, J. (2008) *Working with Babies and Children: From Birth to Three*. London: Sage.

Open University Press/Manchester Metropolitan University (OPU/MMU) (2000) *Shaping the Future Working with the Under Threes*. Professional development pack.

Selleck, D. (2001) 'Being under three years of age: enhancing quality experiences', in G. Pugh (ed.), *Contemporary Issues in the Early Years: Working Collaboratively for Children*. London: Paul Chapman Publishing.

Trevarthen, C. (1977) 'Descriptive analysis of infant communicative behaviour', in H.R. Schaffer (ed.), *Studies in Mother–Infant Interaction*. London: Academic Press.

Trevarthen, C. (2003) 'Infant psychology is an evolving culture', *Human Development*, 46 (4): 233–46.

Wailling, K. (2005) 'What visually attracts two babies: the value of studying babies in their homes and child care settings'. Unpublished MA dissertation, University of Sheffield.

babies' learning and
development

childminding and home childcare

Childminding refers to the practice of childminders being paid to care for children who are not their own, in the childminders home on a regular basis for more than two hours a day.

CHILDMINDING AND HOME CHILDCARERS

Childminding is perhaps the oldest form of childcare – beginning when women shared the care of other women's children. Today, childminders in the UK play a crucial role in the provision of childcare places within the government's National Childcare Strategy and government regulation ensure standards of safety, care and learning opportunities.

In the UK around 500,000 children are cared for by childminders or nannies. For some parents childminding is the preferred option for their child, and the National Childminding Association suggests that there are particular benefits in choosing childminding as a form of care for young children. These include the home environment which can sometimes offer more flexibilty and spontaneity than group day care, including real-life learning experiences such as cooking, shopping, gardening and going to the library. Children are cared for in small groups of children, with mixed ages, so all the children in the family can be with the same carer. Childminding is often a local provision, so children can be cared for in the community where they live and be part of local events and groups. Because childminders usually work in their own homes, hours can be flexible and they can support parents by taking care of older children before and after school, and during school holidays, as well as having younger children during the day.

Registered childminders are required to work according to the Early Years Foundation Stage and are inspected by the Office for Standards in Education (Ofsted) usually every two to three years.

In a large-scale survey of childminders Mooney et al. (2001) found that:

- Childminders were mostly women who chose childminding as a job because it allowed them to combine paid work with caring for their own children.
- A substantial number of childminders see childminding as a long-term career, while others see it as a passing phase of employment.
- Childminders defined themselves as professional childcare workers, but less strongly felt the need for training and qualifications. Personal experience of motherhood was for some an important requirement.
- Childminding demands a variety of skills, not least of which are working within a private market and negotiating relationships with parents. There was a tension between being a carer, with its emphasis on commitment and close personal relationships, and operating as a small business in a private childcare market.
- Although working conditions are poor, childminders recorded high level of satisfaction and commitment to their work.
- Childminders expressed dissatisfaction with what they saw as the low value placed on their work by society. This affected the views of childminders and parents about childminding as an occupation.
- Changes in demographic and employment patterns, regulation and the requirements of childminders are contributing to the fall in the numbers of childminders.

Even in the context of current policy changes which have led to changes in funding of childminding for parents who qualify for it, the above issues form an important set of research issues.

The Northern Ireland Childminding Association (NICA) clarifies its vision as: 'One where all children are cared for, and provided with, the opportunity to learn and develop in a safe, enjoyable home environment and where childminders are recognised and valued as skilled, qualified professionals.'

In New Zealand, the Department of Education identified a need to raise the status of home carers and so made this a political issue. Everiss (2003) describes how the establishment, in 1987, of the New Zealand Family Day Care Association (NZFDCA) and a commissioned government review of family day care, gave a higher status to family day-care providers by providing funding for those caring for children under two years of age. Subsidies were also offered to parents of children under two, regardless of the type of care they selected for their child. Family day carers in New Zealand then found themselves with increased status in the childcare and education field and at the wealthier end of the childcare 'market'. Statutory requirements were put in place to ensure quality, and training for providers entering this aspect of childcare became an area of high demand.

Many childminders are part of informal networks of childminders who support each other and help with holiday cover or in the event of illness. Some childminder networks organise joint activities or events. Children Come First is a quality assurance scheme developed by the National Childminding Association and Ofsted. In Children Come First networks childminders find support according to the needs of the local area from a coordinator who is responsible for assessing and monitoring childminders thus ensuring high-quality provision of care and education.

REFERENCES AND INDICATIVE FURTHER READING

Everiss, E. (2003) 'Family day care in New Zealand: raising the status of the profession', in A. Mooney and J. Stratham (eds), *Family Day Care: International Perspectives on Policy, Practice and Quality*. London: Jessica Kingsley.

Mooney, A., Knight, A., Moss, P. and Owen, C. (2001) *Who Cares? Childminding in the 1990s*. London: Family Policy Studies Centre.

National Childminding Association (2005) *Facts about Childminding and Homecarers*. London: NCMA.

Sure Start (2004) *Thinking About Childminding? Your Questions Answered*. London: Sure Start Unit. Available from Prolog on 0845 60 222 60, or at: www.dfes@prolog.uk.com

children's centres

> *Children's Centres are service hubs where children under five years old and their families can receive seamless integrated services and information.*[1] *Children's Centres offer a wide range of care services encompassing health, education and social care for children under the age of five.*

In the late 1990s the government funded Sure Start initiatives in local communities where services and disciplines combined to improve the learning and development of all children. Health, social services and education facilities combined to provide 'one stop shops' for children and their families. Evaluations of the initiative varied, but a report on the range of activities and success of one of the earliest sure Start Projects in Fox Hill and Parson Cross in Sheffield found that what was offered was greatly valued by parents (Weinberger et al., 2005). The Sure Start Children's Centres have been born out of this earlier Sure Start programme which grew from two in 1997 to 524 Sure Start Local Programmes in 2004 – in the most deprived communities of the country. Combined with neighbourhood nurseries, government statistics indicate that by the end of 2010 there would be 3,500 children's centres – every community would have one, though a subsequent change of government brought uncertainty about this plan.

The UK government's plan that every community would have a local Sure Start Children's Centre by 2010 included the aim that such centres would be locally defined and provision could vary according to local need but would be likely to include:

- integrated early education and childcare – all centres offering Early Years provision have a minimum half-time qualified teacher (increasing to full-time within 18 months of the centre opening);
- support for parents – including advice on parenting, local childcare options and access to specialist services for families;
- child and family health services – ranging from health screening, health visitor services to breast-feeding support;

children's centres

---

[1] http://www.dcsf.gov.uk/everychildmatters/earlyyears/surestart/surestartchildrens centres/childrenscentres/

- helping parents into work – with links to the local Jobcentre Plus and training (DCSF, 2010).

Children's Centres were part of the Labour government's aim that all children should have the opportunity to fulfil their potential. The services provided by children's Centres are designed to help improve outcomes for children as part of the government's ten-year childcare strategy to enable all families with children to have access to an affordable, flexible, high-quality childcare place for their child. The responsibility for estab- lishing the Centres and ensuring they deliver government intentions rests with local authorities. The stated guiding principles are:

1. Working with parents and children. Every family should get access to a range of services that will deliver better outcomes for both children and parents, meeting their needs and stretching their aspirations.
2. Services for everyone. But not the same service for everyone. Families have distinctly different needs, both between different families, in different locations and across time in the same family. Services should recognise and respond to these varying needs.
3. Flexible at point of delivery. All services should be designed to encourage access. For example, opening hours, location, transport issues and care for other children in the family need to be considered. Where possible we must enable families to get the health and family support services they need through a single point of contact.
4. Starting very early. Services for young children and parents should start at the first antenatal visit. This means not only advice on health in pregnancy, but preparation for parenthood, decisions about returning to work (or indeed, starting to work) after the birth, advice on childcare options and on support services available.
5. Respectful and transparent. Services should be customer-driven, whether or not the service is free.
6. Community-driven and professionally coordinated. All professionals with an interest in children and families should be sharing expertise and listening to local people on service priorities. This should be done through consultation and by day-to-day listening to parents.
7. Outcome-driven. All services for children and parents need to have as their core purpose better outcomes for children. The government needs to acknowledge this by reducing bureaucracy and simplifying funding to ensure a joined-up approach with partners (DCSF, 2009).

The change of government in May 2010 and the far reaching cuts in public spending enforced by the incoming Conservative government, threatened the Children's Centre programme. Rudge (2010: 134) considers issues of resources to be a key challenge to the work of Children's Centres:

> Budgets and sustainability are always going to be contentious and, of course, service users will inevitably state the case for more. What clearly is needed is a comprehensive evaluation of how funding is allocated in accordance to what is asked, both in relation to the strategic thinking and the practical application. Children's Centres by their very nature require a holistic approach and as such it is important to note that all disciplines involved with children and families contribute to their success ... A successful Children's Centre is one that has a passion for excellence, a commitment to partnership working, a shared ethos and a flexible approach. While there are many challenges, the potential for Children's Centres is both exciting and substantially beneficial to all concerned, especially for families and children.

REFERENCES AND INDICATIVE FURTHER READING

DCSF (2009) *Sure Start Children's Centres: Our Principles*. Available at: www.dcsf.gov. uk/everychildmatters/earlyyears/surestart/thesurestartprinciples/principles/

DCSF (2010) *Sure Start Children's Centres*. Available at: www.dcsf.gov.uk/everychild-matters/earlyyears/surestart/surestartchildrenscentres/childrenscentres/

Rudge, C. (2010) 'Children's centres', in G. Pugh and B. Duffy (eds), *Contemporary Issues in the Early Years*, 5th edn. London: Sage.

Weinberger, J., Pickstone, C. and Hannon, P. (2005) *Learning from Sure Start: Working with Young Children and their Families*. Buckingham: Open University Press.

> *A citizen is a legally recognized subject or national of a state or commonwealth or an inhabitant of a town or city.[2] With citizenship comes responsibilities, and rights and expectations of ways of behaving within the social group to which the citizen belongs. Thus the notion of children as 'citizens' is sometimes contested.*

Recent changes in curriculum guidance and statutory requirements for provision for children under five have led to an incorporation of curriculum content which might be described as addressing issues of citizenship. For example, the Early Years Foundation Stage (DCSF, 2007) which became statutory in September 2008 states, under what is called 'Positive Relationships: Respecting Each Other' that: 'When each person is valued for who they are and differences are appreciated, everyone feels included and understood, whatever their personality, abilities, ethnic background or culture' (para. 2.1). And in the section identified as 'Enabling Environments: The Learning Environment' is it suggested that: 'When children feel confident in the environment they are willing to try things out, knowing that effort is valued' (para. 3.3). These two statements can be read as clear assertion that inclusion, citizenship and belonging are key to current early years policy in England. But what does 'valuing each child for who they are' look like? And what factors help children to 'feel confident in the environment'?

Though several studies have reported on practitioners' (and other adults') views of inclusion (Clough and Nutbrown, 2004;Cornoldi et al., 1998; Croll and Moses, 2000; Nutbrown and Clough, 2004; Perdue et al., 2001) few studies have considered young children's views of what it is to be included, or to 'belong' to a group, a school, a setting, or a community. Discussing childhood and citizenship in the Israeli context, Ben-Arieh and Boyer (2005: 33) suggest that:

> Citizenship is not merely a formal status … Citizenship is the prerequisite for belonging to a group and as such bears a significant impact on identity formation. Therefore, citizenship is crucial for the well-being of human beings in general and for children in particular. Children's civil status (and

---

[2] *Oxford English Dictionary.*

their citizenship) determines their rights (including their social, political and civil rights).

'Citizenship' has been a modern policy issue for schools in England for more than a decade (QCA, 1998), described for pupils aged 11 years and above as 'Playing a part in society' for the following purpose:

> Citizenship gets pupils working together on issues of concern. It gives them the confidence and skills they need to act with others to tackle real problems in society. They do this by researching and debating complex political, moral and social challenges facing society now and in the future (QCA, 2008: para. 1).

Ben-Arieh and Boyer (2005) agree however, that much less attention has been given to children's citizenship and to the implications such citizenship has for their lives and well-being. Discussing work on citizenship and young people's participation in a civic context, Wyness (2006: 209) claims that:

> International and national political agendas have prioritized children's issues in the past decade or so. However the nature of the commitment to children themselves participating in arrangements that affect them and their communities are highly ambiguous. Whilst children's voices have become progressively louder, the extent to which these voices are articulated within spaces for participation over which children can genuinely claim ownership are often compromised by political structures determined by adults.

Adams's (2005) consideration of the teaching of citizenship in primary schools demonstrates that practical involvement is key to learning to be a citizen and take a view on issues affecting people. In exploring how citizenship might be taught, Anderson (2005) promotes teacher enquiry through the use of fictional texts with children in order to promote thinking around issues of citizenship and responsibility. Whitburn (2003) describes practices in Japanese schools which help young children to be independent and take responsibility, as self-reliant members of a group. She concludes: 'In a densely populated country, I am conscious that "learning to live together" is one of the most important and difficult tasks ahead' (Whitburn, 2003: 175).

In a study of citizenship, belonging and inclusion in pre-school settings, Nutbrown and Clough (2009), give examples of practitioner research

citizenship

projects involving children aged three to six years old. They concluded that (1) children's views can contribute to the development of inclusive practices which are a basis for citizenship, (2) children's voices are central to studies of their perspectives and the methodological challenges of listening to children's voices in research must be addressed, and (3) identity and self-esteem are key to the successful promotion of young children's positive sense of inclusivity and belonging in their early years settings. They argue that including children in the identification and exploration of issues important to them promotes a positive sense of inclusivity and that such approaches to developing pedagogies of citizenship and belonging constitute a practical enacting of 'voice'.

REFERENCES AND INDICATIVE FURTHER READING

Adams, P. (2005) 'Citizenship: how is it different to PSHE and how can it be done?', *Education 3–13*, 33(3): 57–62.

Anderson, B. (2005) 'Can a community of enquiry approach with fiction texts support the development of young pupils' understanding?', *Education 3–13*, 33(3): 9–14.

Ben-Arieh, A. and Boyer, Y. (2005) 'Citizenship and childhood: the state of affairs in Israel', *Childhood*, 12(1): 33–53.

Clough, P. and Nutbrown, C. (2004) 'Special educational needs and inclusive early education: multiple perspectives from UK educators', *Journal of Early Childhood Research*, 2(2): 191– 211.

Cornoldi, C., Terrini, A., Scruggs, T., and Mastropieri, M. (1998) 'Teacher attitudes in Italy after twenty years of inclusion', *Remedial and Special Education*, 19(6): 350–6.

Croll, P. and Moses, D. (2000) 'Ideologies and utopias: education professionals' views of inclusion', *European Journal of Special Needs Education*, 15(1): 1–12.

Department for Children, Schools and Families (DCSF) (2007) *Parents as Partners in Early Learning (PPEL) Project: Parental Involvement – a Snapshot of Policy and Practice PPEL Project Phase 1 Report*. London: DCSF/HMSO.

Nutbrown, C. and Clough, P. (2004) 'Inclusion in the early years: conversations with European educators', *European Journal of Special Needs Education*, 19(3): 311– 39.

Nutbrown, C. and Clough, P. (2009) 'Citizenship and inclusion in the early years: understanding and responding to children's perspectives on "belonging"', *International Journal of Early Years Education*, 17(3): 191–205.

Purdue, K., Ballard, K. and MacArthuer, J. (2001) 'Exclusion and inclusion in New Zealand childhood education: disability, discourses and contexts', *International Journal of Early Years Education*, 9(1): 37–49.

Qualifications and Curriculum Authority (QCA) (1998) *Education for Citizenship and the Teaching of Democracy in Schools*. (The Crick Report.) London: DfEE/QCA.

Whitburn, J. (2003) 'Learning to live together: the Japanese model of early years education', *International Journal of Early Years Education*, 11(2): 155–75.

Wyness, M. (2006) 'Children, young people and civic participation: regulation and local diversity', *Educational Review*, 58(2): 209–18.

developmentally appropriate practice

> *Developmentally Appropriate Practice is the design and development of curriculum and pedagogy based upon agreed stages of children's development. It is a framework of principles and guidelines for best practice in the care and education of young children, birth through age eight.[3]*

In the United States, the National Association for the Education of the Young Child defined 'Developmentally Appropriate Practice' thus:

> ... teachers integrate the many dimensions of their knowledge base. They must know about child development and the implication of this knowledge for how to teach, the content of the curriculum – what to teach and when – how to assess what children have learned, and how to adapt curriculum and instruction to children's individual strengths, needs and interests (NAEYC, 1996).

The term 'developmentally appropriate practice', in the US, is taken to refer to early childhood programmes serving children from birth to eight years. NAEYC documentation states that, in their decision making, effective early childhood educators keep in mind the desired outcomes for children's learning and development, and they understand that:

1. Knowledge must inform decision making
2. Goals must be challenging and achievable
3. Teaching must be intentional to be effective.[4]

The NAEYC proposes the following 12 key principles of child development and learning that inform Developmentally Appropriate Practice:

1. Domains of children's development – physical, social, emotional and cognitive – are closely related. Development in one domain influences and is influenced by development in other domains.

[3]Developmentally Appropriate Practice: www.naeyc.org/DAP
[4]www.naeyc.org/dap/core

2. Development occurs in a relatively orderly sequence, with later abilities, skills and knowledge building on those already acquired.
3. Development proceeds at varying rates from child to child as well as unevenly within different areas of each child's functioning.
4. Early experiences have both cumulative and delayed effects on individual children's development; optimal periods exist for certain types of development and learning.
5. Development proceeds in predictable directions toward greater complexity, organization and internalization.
6. Development and learning occur in and are influenced by multiple social and cultural contexts.
7. Children are active learners, drawing on direct physical and social experience as well as culturally transmitted knowledge to construct their own understandings of the world around them.
8. Development and learning result from interaction of biological maturation and the environment, which includes both the physical and social worlds that children live in.
9. Play is an important vehicle for children's social, emotional and cognitive development, as well as a reflection of their development.
10. Development advances when children have opportunities to practice newly acquired skills as well as when they experience a challenge just beyond the level of their present mastery.
11. Children demonstrate different modes of knowing and learning and different ways of representing what they know.
12. Children develop and learn best in the context of a community where they are safe and valued, their physical needs are met, and they feel psychologically secure (NAEYC, 2009: 10–16).

Katz suggests that in developmentally appropriate approaches to curriculum decisions 'about what should be learned and how it would best be learned depend on what we know of the learner's developmental status and our understanding of the relationships between early experience and subsequent development' (1995: 109).

Herein lie the questions for research. How can educators know what *should* be learned? How are decisions taken about what next to teach? How are children's stages of development determined? How can educators understand the connections between early experience and later development?

Of course, views of *development* and what constitutes *appropriate* development are always contestable. However, taken together with Vygotsky's notion of the *zone of proximal development* it is possible to identify ways in which supporting children's learning can be informed and appropriate to their stage of learning.

Such questions have underpinned many studies which have sought to inform curriculum and programme development: for example, Athey's (2007) work on schematic development; Nutbrown's study of curriculum development based on schematic theory (2006); Reggio Emilia pre-school's development of communities of learning through multiple modes of expression (Abbott and Nutbrown, 2001; Edwards et al., 2001; Malaguzzi, 1996) and the curriculum *Te Whāriki* developed in New Zealand – a policy which promotes equality of opportunity in contexts of diversity (Ministry of Education New Zealand, 1995). Such studies and policy developments are evidence of the continuing quest for ways of creating curriculum which satisfactorily meet the developmental needs of young children – internationally.

The following examples demonstrate the wide range of practices which can be identified as developmentally appropriate and, of course, the extent to which such practices are developmentally appropriate is always a matter of judgement. Such judgements can only usually be determined when the details of context and history are available.

In a study of baby signing, Johnston (2005: 137) recorded the progress of babies and demonstrated how they could communicate with their Key Person. Unsurprisingly the examples describe the babies' eating and drinking patterns and preferences, and show the ability to sign helps the practitioner to meet the babies' developmental needs.

Mark's story

Mark's first sign was 'milk', I took his milk out of the fridge and I asked him 'do you want some milk Mark?' and I showed him the sign for 'milk', as I always do. On this occasion Mark started to imitate the sign, we praised Mark, he was very excited and he laughed.

Although we are doing lots of signs with Mark he watches and concentrates so intently, he is not yet picking any of the signs up. However Mark is playing with sounds and can copy many words such as 'hiya', 'tiger' and 'spider'. We do the signs for these words too.

Mark had finished his dinner and I asked 'have you finished Mark?' I showed him the sign for 'finished'. Mark laughed and waved his hands in the air, Mark's attempt was great and we gave him lots of praise even though he did not complete the correct sign.

Mark did the sign for 'milk' this morning as soon as he arrived at nursery; I asked Mark's mother if he had drunk any milk yet this morning. Mark's mother explained that he had not yet had any milk and she had brought an extra bottle. I warmed some milk up for Mark and we sat down together, Mark drank the whole bottle of milk and we had a big cuddle. Mark was able to communicate his need this morning.

Mark has been attempting to smack his friends and some of the practitioners; we tell Mark 'no thank you' and show him the sign for 'no'. Mark stops immediately – he understands the word for 'no' and the sign, although he cannot copy it.

Mark is able to copy the sign for 'drink'; he usually does this sign when he is eating his dinner, however he does sometimes do it while he is playing. Drinks are available throughout the day and not just when they ask for them.

While the practitioner Pam was helping Mark to eat his dinner, Pam asked him 'do you want some more Mark?' Pam showed him the sign for 'more'. Mark put his hands together and successfully completed the sign he then started clapping he was so proud of himself. Mark can now do this sign competently, one of the other children was sharing some of their chocolate raisins with Mark, as soon as Mark ate one he carried on doing the sign for 'more'.

I was showing Mark the sign for 'Daddy', because his daddy was picking him up. Mark was able to do the sign and say the word. Mark completed this sign lots and was able to do the sign once his Daddy arrived. After mastering the sign for 'Daddy' we have been showing Mark the sign for 'Mummy'. Mark is able to do a very similar sign to the correct one.

I asked Mark 'where's the birdies?' I showed him the sign for 'bird'. I took Mark to the gate and opened the door so we could see the garden. There was a bird on the grass so I said 'birdie'. Mark was really excited by this, on another occasion I could see him sitting on the floor by the gate doing the sign for 'bird', he had spotted a bird outside, I went over and said 'bird'. Mark was so thrilled he stood up at the gate; he was laughing and still doing the sign for 'bird'.

Mark walked into the bathroom and did the sign for 'change'. I was interested to know if Mark associated the sign with the bathroom or if he needed changing. I checked his nappy and his nappy was soiled. I asked Mark 'shall we change your nappy?' Mark lifted his arms up so I could lift him onto the changing mat and I changed his nappy for him.

Continuous provision planning

Staff of the community playgroup had recently attended a workshop on the role of the key person and strategies for planning the environment more effectively. Before attending the training the practitioners of the pre-school had struggled to organise their environment to show differentiation for the children aged between two–two and half in their group. The older children seemed to be catered for quite well.

Following the training, and with further support from their birth to three consultant, the setting worked toward implementing the key person approach. They adopted and adapted the 'Continuous Provision Planning Sheet' paying careful attention to ensure that they recorded children's initials and their individual interests in a simple manner. They needed a document that could be updated regularly to differentiate learning intentions according to the needs and abilities of each child in order to plan for their next experiences. This simple but effective tool ensured that the offered curriculum was available to all the children and meaningful connections to observations of individual children. The dated documents provided records of children's individuality and progression which meant that the setting was able to dispense with their previous, often meaningless, tick list.

Two months later the setting had an unannounced Ofsted inspection and practitioners were delighted to receive an overall judgement grade of 'Outstanding'. The inspector made particular note of the way practitioners had used their observations and assessment of the youngest children to support their sensitive and appropriate planning. The practitioners reflected upon the changes they had made and positive effect on the quality of the children's experience. They recorded their findings in their Ofsted Self Evaluation Form as evidence to support their development and continuous improvement.

When the setting received its final report, staff were very pleased to see that the Inspector had acknowledged their recent training, noting its particular impact on their understanding and ultimate outcomes for children.
(Nutbrown and Page, 2008: 85)

Jenkinson writes of the crucial role of play in children's development and how one teacher combined the requirement to give young children homework with the importance of finding time for children to play. Jenkinson wrote:

A teacher colleague of mine working in London was so concerned about her class's lack of ability to play that for their homework she told them to go home and build a den. They announced to their surprised parents, 'Mrs Ginn says we've got to make dens'. Mattresses were dragged from beds, chairs and tables upturned, sheets were draped everywhere, and a crop of dens sprung up like mushrooms. The children enjoyed themselves tremendously, and were far livelier in their work as a result. Order was restored to the various homes, although the children were keen to repeat their experience.

One den, which deserves special mention for ingenuity and charm, was erected in a small garden. An inspired and generous adult gave the children a meringue-shaped wedding dress to play with. Using clothes pegs, the children suspended the frothy white garment between the washing line and the bushes, creeping under the satin to play in secret bliss beneath the white lacy roof of their exotic pavilion. (Jenkinson, 2001: 137–8)

REFERENCES AND INDICATIVE FURTHER READING

Abbott, L. and Nutbrown, C. (eds) (2001) *Experiencing Reggio Emilia: Implications for Preschool Provision*. Milton Keynes: Open University Press.

Athey, C. (2007) *Extending Thought in Young Children*. London: Sage.

Bredekamp, S. (1991) *Developmentally Appropriate Practice*. New York: NAEYC.

David, T. (1996) 'Their right to play', in C. Nutbrown (ed.), *Respectful Educators – Capable Learners: Children's Rights and Early Education*. London: Paul Chapman Publishing.

Edwards, G., Gandini, L. and Forman, G. (eds) (2001) *The Hundred Languages of Children – The Reggio Emilia Approach to Early Childhood Education*, 2nd edn. Norwood, NJ: Ablex.

Gestwicki, C. (1998) *Developmentally Appropriate Practice: Curriculum and Development in Early Education*, 2nd edn. New York: Delmar.

Jenkinson, S. (2001) *The Genius of Play*. Stroud: Hawthorn Press.

Johnston, A. (2005) *Who benefits from baby signing?*, unpublished MA dissertation, University of Sheffield.

Katz, L. (1995) *Talks with Teachers of Young Children: A Collection*. Norwood, NJ: Ablex.

Malaguzzi, L. (1996) 'The right to environment', in T. Filippini and V. Vecchi (eds), *The Hundred Languages of Children: The Exhibit*. Reggio Emilia: Reggio Children.

Ministry of Education New Zealand (1995) *Te Whāriki – Guidelines for Developmentally Appropriate Programmes in Early Childhood Services*. Learning Media Ltd, Box 3293, Wellington, NZ.

NAEYC (1996) *Guidelines for Decisions about Developmentally Appropriate Practice*. Available at: www.naeyc.org/about/position/dap4.htm

NAEYC (2009) *Position Statement: Developmentally Appropriate Practice in Early Childhood Programs Serving Children from Birth through Age 8*. Available at: www.naeyc.org/DAP

Nutbrown, C. (2006) *Threads of Thinking: Young Children Learning and the Role of Early Education*, 3rd edn. London: Sage.

Nutbrown, C. and Page, J. (2008) *Working with Babies and Children: From Birth to Three*. London: Sage.

Technologies developed in recent decades have facilitated instant communication through digital and electronic means, including: personal
computers, the Internet, digital games, personal games devices, mobile
phones and other personal communication devices.

The technological age of the late twentieth and early twenty-first centuries
brought with it radical change which impacted on almost every aspect
of life in many parts of the world and early childhood education, and
care was no exception. These changes have provided equipment for
work and leisure of adults and the education and play of young children
which has surpassed any possible imagining. Literacy, for example, is no
longer just a case of putting pen to paper, but increasingly of putting
fingers to keyboard or stroking touch screens, and reading material is
not only available in a static printed form but also in fluid forms on
computer and electronic monitors – leading to new definitions of
literacy (Barton and Hamilton, 1998). New digital technologies have
transformed the toy market leading to 'interactive toys' and media
technology designed especially for young children (Emory et al.,
2000). With the increase in digital technological toys and equipment
produced for and marketed at young children, early years practitioners,
researchers and parents have, necessarily, focused on how digital technologies can be used with young children and how such use might
affect (either positively or negatively) their learning and development.
Whatever the beliefs and practices of adults, the changing culture of
many children's childhoods is inescapable and, for many, it is very
different from the childhoods of their parents or teachers (Luke and
Luke, 2001).

In parallel with the growth of new digital technologies has come a
growth of research interests which seems to span a 'for and against'
continuum. Some studies seek to identify good practice in incorporating
digital technologies in early years settings and positively exploit their
use in order to support children's learning and development, while others
raise awareness of the potential harm which overuse of technology can
cause and even call for the elimination of digital technnologies in the

early years. Inevitably, there arises from such a continuum of extreme opinion, numerous research issues.

O'Hara (2004) argues for a developmentally appropriate use of information and communication technology (ICT) in early years settings and the integration of ICT into the curriculum with appropriate pedagogy. The place of ICT, and its appropriate use, in young children's learning and development remains an issue for research. Siraj-Blatchford and Whitebread (2003) acknowledge concerns around ICT and young children, and discuss ways in which ICT in the early years can be compatible with the principles of a Developmentally Appropriate Curriculum (DAC). They argue that imaginative use of ICT can ensure that it supports the unique development of young children, both socially and cognitively.

The Alliance for Childhood (US) in a report called *Fool's Gold* which highlighted the dangers of computers in childhood, made seven key recommendations which could form an agenda for future research:

1. A refocusing in education, at home and school, on the essentials of a healthy childhood: strong bonds with caring adults; time for spontaneous, creative play; a curriculum rich in music and the other arts; reading books aloud; storytelling and poetry; rhythm and movement; cooking, building things, and other handcrafts; and gardening and other hands-on experiences of nature and the physical world.
2. A broad public dialogue on how emphasizing computers is affecting the real needs of children, especially children in low-income families.
3. A comprehensive report by the US Surgeon General on the full extent of physical, emotional, and other developmental hazards computers pose to children.
4. Full disclosure by information technology companies about the physical hazards to children of using their products.
5. A halt to the commercial hyping of harmful or useless technology for children.
6. A new emphasis on ethics, responsibility, and critical thinking in teaching older students about the personal and social effects of technology.
7. An immediate moratorium on the further introduction of computers in early childhood and elementary education, except for special cases of students with disabilities. Such a time out is necessary to create the climate for the above recommendations to take place (Cordes and Miller, 2000: 98).

In a later report, *Tech Tonic: Towards a New Literacy of Technology* the Alliance for Childhood sets out three central concerns which, again, form a potential research agenda:

1. Children face a daunting technological frontier of irreversible changes in human biology and the world's ecology. They need a radically different kind of technology education to make wise choices in such a future.
2. Children's lives are increasingly filled with screen time rather than real time with nature, caring adults, the arts, and hands-on work and play. Yet only real relationships, not virtual ones, will inspire and prepare them to protect the Earth and all that lives on it.
3. There is scant evidence of long-term benefits – and growing indications of harm – from the high-technology lifestyle and education aggressively promoted by government and business. It is time for concerted citizen action to reclaim childhood for children (Alliance for Childhood, 2004).

Sheridan and Samuelsson-Pramling (2003) point out that 'Sweden has enthusiastically adopted the technology and in the process has become a world leader, in terms of numbers of computers per capita and frequency of Internet use (Next Generation Forum, 1999, 2000)'. In their examination of ICT and young children Sheridan and Samuelsson-Pramling (2003: 15) set a clear research agenda:

> Although ICT is strongly related to learning, there is no self-evident connection between access to technology, changes in working methods, and improved learning for the children ... Therefore, the following questions need to be raised: What are the conditions that would allow ICT to become a tool for the kind of learning that is the goal of preschool and school curricula? Can ICT be used in preschool and beyond to create alternative scenarios, thereby making it possible for a child to discern something he otherwise would not have? How do such factors as teachers' education, competency, and pedagogical beliefs concerning ICT and younger children affect the likelihood of children becoming skillful users of ICT? And why are these technological skills important for young children to acquire?

Digital technologies have the power to change learning, and Green et al. (2005) have set out a learner's charter – describing how digital technologies can be used to enhance personalised learning for children from three to

16 years of age. In it they show how all aspects of learning can be enhanced through appropriate use of digital technologies:

> This charter has been designed to stimulate debate around how digital technologies and institutional change might enable personalisation in four key areas (the more familiar terms to which these areas relate are in brackets):
>
> - choices (learner voice and choice)
> - skills and knowledge (curriculum)
> - learning environments (pedagogies and institutions)
> - feedback (assessment and recognition). (Green et al., 2005: 6)

Some schools use blogs to good effect, using digital media as an integral part of the curriculum. Examples from Monteney School in Sheffield, for example, show how children have explored issues of internet usage, and have developed numerous skills, including: interviewing, blog and filmmaking to post their projects on their school blog (monteney.sheffield.sch.uks/monteney/bloghome.htm). The Digital Beginnings Project (Marsh et al., 2005) explored young children's (aged from birth to six) use of popular culture, media and new technologies in the home through a survey of 1,852 parents and carers of children who attended 120 individual maintained and non-maintained early years settings in England. The many key findings included the following:

1. Young children are immersed in practices relating to popular culture, media and new technologies from birth. They are growing up in a digital world and develop a wide range of skills, knowledge and understanding of this world from birth. Parents and other family members scaffold this learning, either implicitly or explicitly, and children engage in family social and cultural practices which develop their understanding of the role of media and technology in society.
2. Parents report that their young children generally lead well-balanced lives, with popular culture, media and new technologies playing an important, but not overwhelming role in their leisure activities. Engagement with media is generally active, not passive, and promotes play, speaking and listening and reading. In addition, engagement with media and new technologies appears to be a primarily social, not individual, activity, taking place most often with other family members and in shared parts of living spaces.

3. Parents are generally very positive about the role of media in their young children's social, emotional, linguistic and cognitive development. They feel that their children learn a great deal from film and television and that it has a positive impact on many aspects of their lives.

4. Parents support their children's interest in popular culture, media and new technologies through the provision of resources and interactions with children (for example, shared play, visits to theme parks) around their interests. Parents feel that media education should be included in the school curriculum; many think this should be so from when children are very young. Parents would also welcome further work in schools on new technologies. They feel that this is needed in order to prepare children for the demands of the new technological age (Marsh et al., 2005: 5).

The Digital Beginnings Project made a number of recommendations for practice, including the need for professional development for early years practitioners; some settings need financial support to acquire the necessary technology in order to enhance the curriculum; family involvement could be further exploited to maximise synergy between home and settings; and content producers (television, and film companies) could work more closely with early years educators in designing support materials and so on. Finally – the report concludes that: 'many young children demonstrate a wide range of skills and knowledge in relation to technologies' (Marsh et al., 2005: 8).

REFERENCES AND INDICATIVE FURTHER READING

Alexandersson, M. and Samuelsson-Pramling, I. (1998) 'New ways of learning. A project focusing how children learn through IT', project application to the Swedish National Agency for Higher Education, Stockholm.

Alliance for Childhood (2004) *Tech Tonic: Towards a New Literacy of Technology.* College Park, MD: Alliance for Childhood. Available at www.allianceforchildhood. org and P.O. Box 444 College Park, MD 20741.

Barton, D. and Hamilton, M. (1998) *Local Literacies: Reading and Writing in One Community.* London: Routledge.

Cordes, C. and Miller, E. (eds) (2000) *Fool's Gold: A Critical Look at Computers in Childhood.* College Park, MD: Alliance for Childhood.

Emory, H., Woodard, I. and Gridina, N. (2000) 'Media in the Home 2000: The Fifth Annual Survey of Parents and Children', Annenberg Public Policy Center of the University of Pennsylvania.

Green, H., Facer, K. and Rudd, T., with Dillon, P. and Humphreys, P. (2005) *Personalisation and Digital Technologies.* Bristol: Futurelab.

Luke, A. and Luke, C. (2001) 'Adolescence lost/childhood regained: on early intervention and the emergence of the techno-subject', *Journal of Early Childhood Literacy*, 1(1): 91–120.

Marsh, J., Brooks, G., Hughes, J., Ritchie, L., Roberts, S. and Wright, K. (2005) *Digital Beginnings: Young Children's Use of Popular Culture, Media and New Technologies: Report of the 'Young Children's Use of Popular Culture, Media and New Technologies' Study, Funded by BBC Worldwide and the Esmée Fairbairn Foundation*. Sheffield: Literacy Research Centre, University of Sheffield. Available at: www.digitalbeginnings.shef.ac.uk/final-report.htm

Marsh, M. (2004) 'The techno-literacy practices of young children', *Journal of Early Childhood Research*, 2(1): 51–66.

Marsh, M. (2010) 'Young children's play in online virtual worlds', *Journal of Early Childhood Research*, 8(1): 23–39.

Next Generation Forum (1999) *Toward the Creative Society. Next Generation Annual Report 1999*. Kopenhamn: Next Generation Forum.

Next Generation Forum (2000) 'Next Generation Annual Report 2000, first draft', fourth Next Generation roundtable meeting, Costa Rica, June.

O'Hara, M. (2004) *ICT in the Early Years*. London: Continuum.

Sheridan, S. and Samuelsson-Pramling, I. (2003) 'Learning through ICT in Swedish Early Childhood Education from a pedagogical perspective of quality', *Childhood Education*, 79(5): 276– 92.

Siraj-Blatchford, J. and Whitebread, D. (2003) *Supporting ICT in the Early Years*. Buckingham: Open University Press.

Yeland, N. (2005) 'Curriculum, pedagogies and practice in ICT in the information age', in N. Yelland (ed.), *Critical Issues in Early Childhood Education*. Buckingham: Open University Press.

key concepts in early childhood education and care

early intervention studies

Early Intervention is the term often used to describe programmes and strategies in early education which are designed to make a difference to children's later educational achievement.

The belief that the early years are crucial to children's later educational achievement and, in some cases, to their social, emotional and physical development, has prompted the development of programmes, techniques and strategies which target young children who are 'at risk' in some way. Such programmes are designed to make a difference to children's later educational achievement. Early Intervention programmes are based on the premise that 'beginning early' means a greater chance of being successful and are often designed to prevent difficulties as well as to seek to overcome any difficulties which young children already have.

Early Intervention programmes and strategies are fuelled by the existence of deep inequalities in many societies and such programmes have to go further than simply providing access to early childhood education or care. Making it possible to attend some form of pre-school provision often misses the most vulnerable groups, and can fail to provide the necessary support for children who are vulnerable or at risk of later school failure. The National Child Development Study (NCDS) began with data from 15,000 children all born within the same week in the UK in 1958. In the seven-year follow-up it was found that the children's teachers judged far more children whose parents were unskilled or semi-skilled manual workers to have special educational needs (24 per cent and 17 per cent) than children whose parents were in professional groups (4 per cent and 7 per cent) (Davie et al., 1972). The same NCDS sample was studied at age 11 and found 6 per cent of the 11 year olds were 'disadvantaged' – that is, living in single-parent or large families and in families with low income and poor housing. This 6 per cent were some three and a half years behind their peers according to reading tests and more likely to be receiving additional teaching support due to learning difficulties (Wedge and Prosser, 1973).

Educational disadvantage is still linked, with some concern, to other factors such as housing, poverty, parents' educational qualifications and so on. The Sure Start Programme in the UK can be seen as a large-scale Early Intervention programme which sought to address multiple factors which threaten children's development. Such programmes seek to provide something specific and additional to usual mainstream provision, are often targeted at groups most likely to benefit, and aim to change something. Many parenting programmes designed to support parents in managing their toddler's behaviour are Early Intervention Programmes with the aim of bringing about a change in the child's behaviour as a result of the parent changing his or her behaviour.

Since the 1960s there have been several well-known Early Intervention Programmes such as the High Scope Perry Preschool Project (Schweinhart et al., 1993, 2004; Whitehurst et al., 1994). In New Zealand, the Reading Recovery programme was designed to enhance the reading development of children, who, at around six years old, were below their peers in terms of assessed reading attainment. Reading Recovery has since been used in many countries as a short-term programme whereby children are 'discontinued' and return to usual teaching programmes as soon as they reach an acceptable level of achievement as assessed on a number of tests (Clay, 1972).

The crucial research issue in relation to early intervention is effectiveness. How can we know that Early Intervention Programmes and strategies will achieve their aims? This is a key question for research, but such studies require funding, and the necessary methodology can be complex and the process costly. Bronfenbrenner (1974) reviewed findings of 26 experimental Early Intervention studies and reported on findings from two types of programme: 'group' and 'parent–child'. Bronfenbrenner's review showed that programmes involving parents had longer lasting effects than those which only provided for or worked with the child. He concluded that programmes which addressed all the factors which contribute to educational failure should be developed in the future. It is just this strategy that underpinned the Sure Start programmes which sought to support children's learning and development *alongside* strategies to tackle difficulties in families and their communities which militate against healthy progress in childhood.

In the UK there have been few experimental studies which have been designed adequately to evaluate the impact of experimental Early Intervention Programmes. One example of such a study is the Raising Early Achievement in Literacy (REAL) Project (Nutbrown et al., 2005). This study (which took place between 1995 and 2003) brought together the university, the local education authority and many Sheffield schools with the aim of promoting family literacy through work with parents of pre-school children. From the outset the project had six main aims:

1. To develop methods of working with parents to promote the literacy development of pre-school children (particularly those likely to have difficulties in the early years of school).
2. To meet some of the literacy and educational needs of the parents so involved.
3. To ensure the *feasibility* of methods developed.
4. To assess the *effectiveness* of the methods in improving children's literacy development at school entry and afterwards.
5. To disseminate effective methods to practitioners and to equip them with new skills.
6. To inform policy-makers about the effectiveness and implications of new practices.

The most promising methods developed in phase 1 were used to develop an 18-month 'long duration, low intensity' early literacy programme of work with families. Based on the ORIM framework (Figure 5, p. 105), the programme had five main components: home visits by programme teachers; provision of literacy resources (particularly books); centre-based group activities; special events (e.g. group library visits); postal communication between teacher and child. The core of the programme was similar at all schools but shaped by local community circumstances and teachers' styles. A total of 80 families from those ten schools (eight families working with each teacher) participated in the programme. Teachers were funded for release one half-day per week to work with the families in their group. Adult learning opportunities for parents were also developed and offered to parents. Outcomes in terms of measures of children's literacy showed that the programme was effective in making a difference to children's literacy with children in the programme scoring more highly than children in control groups. Nutbrown et al. (2005) report that the programme was highly valued by parents who were involved in their children's literacy and by programme teachers.

They also report on children's enhanced achievement in literacy. Children reported that their parents, (mothers *and* fathers) were involved in their home literacy (Morgan et al., 2009; Nutbrown and Hannon, 2003).

REFERENCES AND INDICATIVE FURTHER READING

Bronfenbrenner, U. (1974) *A Report on Longitudinal Evaluations of Preschool Programs. Vol 2. Is Early Intervention Effective?* Washington, DC: DHEW.

Clay, M. (1972) *Reading Recovery: The Patterning of Complex Behaviour.* Auckland: Heinemann.

Davie, R., Butler, N. and Goldstein, H. (1972) *From Birth to Seven: A Report of the National Child Development Study.* London: Longman.

Feldman, M. (ed.) (2004) *Early Intervention: The Essential Readings.* Oxford: Blackwell.

Morgan, A., Nutbrown, C. and Hannon, P. (2009) 'Fathers' involvement in young children's literacy development: implications for family literacy programmes', *British Educational Research Journal*, 35(2):167–85.

Nutbrown, C. and Hannon, P. (2003) 'Children's perspectives on early literacy: issues and methodologies', *Journal of Early Childhood Literacy*, 3(2): 115–45.

Nutbrown, C., Hannon, P. and Morgan, A. (2005) *Early Literacy Work With Families: Policy, Practice and Research.* London: Sage.

Schweinhart, L.J., Barnes, H.V. and Weikart, D.P. (1993) *Significant Benefits: The High Scope Perry Preschool Study through age 27.* Monograph of the High Scope Educational Research Foundation. Ypsilanti, MI: High Scope Press.

Schweinhart, L.J., Montie, J., Xiang, Z., Barnett, W.S., Belfield, C.R. and Nores, M. (2004) *Lifetime Effects: The High Scope Perry Preschool Study through Age 40.* Monograph of the High Scope Educational Research Foundation. Ypsilanti, MI: High Scope Press.

Wedge, P. and Prosser, H. (1973) *Born to Fail?* London: Arrow Books/National Children's Bureau.

Whitehurst, G.J., Epstein, J.N., Angell, A.L., Payne, D.A., Crone, D.A. and Fischel, J.E. (1994) 'Outcomes of an emergent literacy intervention in Head Start', *Journal of Educational Psychology*, 86(4): 542–55.

early literacy development

Early literacy development is the term used to refer to the ways in which young children acquire understanding, skills and knowledge related to aspects of early literacy such as using books, early writing, using environmental print and aspects of oral language.

Until the 1970s early literacy development was largely overlooked. Nursery education tended to focus on oral language and story telling. Literacy became part of the early years curriculum during the 1980s with the growth of research in *emergent literacy* and a shift from a belief that literacy learning too young could be harmful to the development of practices which incorporated meaningful literacy activities which reflected children's everyday lives, into the curriculum. New ways of teaching literacy were developed during the 1980s as researchers and teachers became more aware of *how* children learned about writing and reading. These changes in thinking and practice were also incorporated (to some extent) in the new English National Curriculum in 1988 (DES, 1988). In the two decades since then, developments have continued with rapidity and it is now rare to find settings where literacy is not fully incorporated into the curriculum and children encouraged to use reading and writing in many aspects of their play. The Early Years Foundation Stage (DCSF, 2008) promoted the incorporation of aspects of literacy learning through play and required the assessment of literacy according to children's knowledge, skills and abilities in communication, language and literacy.

It can be helpful to consider some main strands of early literacy development which research suggests are important. In a major family literacy programme involving parents and young children, the following 'strands' were identified: environmental print, books, early writing and key aspects of oral language (Nutbrown et al., 2005).

Early literacy is an area rich in research, with key studies in environmental print, books, early writing and aspects of oral languages being the subjects of international studies.

ENVIRONMENTAL PRINT

In countries where print abounds there is no shortage of examples, commercial print of all kinds can be found on clothing, buildings, packaging, household equipment, and so on. It may be temporary and ever-changing as with electronic billboards and digital screens on shopping centres, cars and transport depots (bus and rail stations and airports for example). Context-based print, such as that found on household packaging and shop signs, is meaningful to young children and has a place in their reading development as children draw meaning from familiar symbols in their environment (Goodman et al., 1978; Hiebert, 1981). It has been suggested that reading begins the moment young children become aware of environmental print (Smith, 1976) and many children develop a sense of such print awareness long before going to school (Burke, 1982; Goodman, 1980). Environmental print can stimulate talk about literacy as children ask questions such as 'What does that say?' It also prompts children, at times, to pick out and identify from signs, some letters that are familiar to them, perhaps in their own name. Environmental print can stimulate some children to write; children often imitate the writing they see, such as notices or notes left for others.

BOOKS

Access to books, especially good quality books, both children's fiction and non-fiction material, is essential if children are to build a good foundation of reading in their early years. Concepts such as the quality of illustration or the overall quality of the story and look of a book are matters for personal judgements but if children are introduced to books that are among the best in children's publishing they are more likely to want to use them, to turn the pages, to look at the pictures and listen to the story, and to return to the book again later.

Children absorb messages very quickly, both positive and negative, and so the literature offered to children and taken into homes needs to be selected so that it offers positive images of all members of society, of a variety of cultures and of both male and female. The first encounter with a particular book is important, and the cover, the feel, size, shape as well as content make a difference to whether children and parents are attracted to read it or not. Meek (1982) argued that reading books and stories *together* is the fundamental cornerstone of reading. In recent years there has been a growth of literature for children based on the popular culture of the time. Books related to children's television programmes and films abound, and numerous related comics for children are available in most newsagents. Marsh (2005) has argued that literacy related to children's popular culture should be valued and children's use of texts in comics, film and TV-related story books, television and other multimedia literacies should be a part of children's literacy repertoires.

EARLY WRITING

Some studies the writing of researchers' own children (Baghban, 1984; Bissex, 1980; Payton, 1984; Schickedanz, 1990) have resulted in a useful bank of material which can be used to examine the fine detail of children's early literacy achievements and patterns of learning. Research into children's early mark-making (Ferrerio and Teberosky, 1989; Goodman, 1980; Harste et al., 1984; Ross and Brondy, 1987) challenged the earlier belief that children could not and should not write until they go to school. As more was understood about 'emergent' or 'developmental' writing, teachers in the early years began to watch what children were doing and incorporate provision and support for such writing behaviours and interests into the pre-school curriculum. Ferrerio and Teberosky's (1989) work focused on the hypotheses about writing which children generated for themselves as they tried to understand writing rules and conventions. They argue that *writing is not copying an external model*. The children in their study explored various ideas and hypotheses about writing – writing, they argue, does not depend on graphic skill (their ability to make letters look conventional) but on the level of conceptualisation about writing – that is, the set of hypotheses they have explored for the purpose of understanding writing. Figure 2 (p. 46) suggests a model of thinking about how young children make sense of writing through three processes:

ORAL LANGUAGE (STORYTELLING, PHONOLOGICAL AWARENESS, TALK ABOUT LITERACY)

Three aspects of oral language appear to be key to children's literacy learning and development: storytelling, phonological awareness and 'talk about literacy'.

Observation	Children see other people writing and using writing for everyday purposes: family members, people in the community and staff in education and care settings
Interaction	Children are involved in writing interchanges with adults who write alongside them: birthday cards, letters, order forms, quick notes; some adults sometimes directly 'tutor' the children in how to write
Representation	Children make their own graphic marks which gradually become more conventional in appearance as their skills develop and knowledge about writing increases, and as they try to represent the actions and products of writers and learn more about writing that enables them to develop the skills they need

Figure 2 *A model of how young children make sense of writing through three processes (Nutbrown, 1997: 34)*

Phonological awareness

Studies by Goswami and Bryant (1990) and Maclean et al. (1987) have helped to pinpoint the importance of *phonological awareness* in children's literacy development. Goswami and Bryant (1990) suggested that the important thing for children to be aware of is what they call *onset* and *rime* in spoken words, 'onset' being the beginning sound and 'rime' being the end sound of a word. Words like 'stroke', 'stripe', 'strum', strip' share the same *onset* and so they are said to *alliterate*. Words such as 'wing', 'thing' 'ring', 'bring' share the same *rime* and can be said to *rhyme*. Goswami and Bryant (1990) present substantial evidence from their studies of pre-school children which suggests that children who are aware of onset and rime find learning to read easier. They show how pre-school tests of this kind of phonological awareness predict reading attainment later, and how pre-school 'training' to help children detect onset and rime can boost later reading attainment. Maclean et al. (1987) found that pre-school children's knowledge of nursery rhymes predicted later reading success in school.

Storytelling

Well's (1987) longitudinal study suggested that the best predictor of children's reading attainment in school was a measure of what he termed 'knowledge of literacy' at school entry. Other simple measures of literacy, such as whether a child can name a favourite book (Weinberger, 1996) have also been found to be powerful predictors of later reading achievement. It is likely that this type of literacy knowledge at school entry is acquired as a result of other important things happening in the pre-school years. Well's study of children's language in the home identified key experiences. These were: *listening* to a story told; other sharing of picture books; drawing and colouring and early writing. Foremost of all these activities was *listening to stories read aloud* which stood out above all the others as being related to the 'knowledge of literacy' measure and later test scores. Wells suggested that the reason for this centred around the various benefits children gain from listening to stories: experience of a genre later encountered in written form; extension of experience and vocabulary; increased conversation with adults; children's own 'inner storying' validated; experience of language use to *create worlds*; and insight into *storying* as a means of understanding.

Talk about literacy

Written language can form an important part of the lives of pre-school children, with some noticing a great deal of print around them and some will be aware that the adults around them use print a great deal in their everyday lives. It is therefore quite natural for children in these situations to be curious about print, to ask questions and, from time to time, to want to talk about the print they see – just as they do about other things that are of interest to them. Children's vocabularies grow at an astonishing rate in the pre-school years and some of the new words they acquire could well be words which relate to literacy. Research continues to be carried out on how children learn literacy and how best it can be taught. Most recently the place of new media and popular culture in children's early literacy development has attracted research interest, with several studies reported in the *Journal of Early Literacy Research*.

The following account describes one teacher's project, to promote writing at home between parents and children.

Developing a home–school writing project

The project started with an initial information meeting, the aim of which was to inform parents of the progression they could expect to see as their

Table 2   A four-week home–school writing programme

Week	Focus
1	Teddy wrote a letter to his/her new friend and the children each wrote a reply
2	Teddy invited his/her friend to his/her birthday party. Each child wrote a reply
3	Writing a shopping list for the birthday party
4	Teddy's birthday party! The children made and wrote birthday cards for their teddy.

children experimented with mark making. I wanted to share with parents the importance of letting their children 'have a go' rather than writing everything for them to copy.

I used slides of progressive examples of children's independent writing to illustrate the points I was making. I also emphasised the importance of the fact that children develop at different rates and what was important was that children developed the confidence to have a go. Parents could become involved in this process by providing meaningful opportunities for writing and children would have the opportunity to develop their skills and become confident writers.

The project ran over four weeks and revolved around a teddy bear! To begin with all the children were given a teddy along with a selection of writing materials. Each week parents had the opportunity to come to school on either a Tuesday or Wednesday morning and see me modelling the weekly writing task. This was followed by the parents working with their children on the writing task with me and the nursery nurse on hand to offer help or guidance. Every Friday the teddies went home, along with another writing task which was similar to the task completed in school during the week. This ensured that all the parents had an opportunity to be involved in the project if they wanted to, even if they could not get to the weekly sessions in school. Table 2 shows the programme.

Outcomes and achievements

The children and parents became very involved in the project. In total, 17 out of 30 children had their parent or grandparent come into school to work with them and almost everyone in the class worked at home on the weekly task.

As a result of the project it was possible to see how children developed as confident writers who were prepared to have a go. Parents were now more aware of how they could encourage their children as independent writers rather than dismissing their independent attempts and writing things for the children to copy a more perfect form. Parents were also trying to find ways of involving their children in meaningful writing tasks at home.

The project emphasised the importance of providing parents with the necessary information to enable them to work effectively with their children. I am looking forward to developing an annual programme of work with parents that will enable them to work with their children in other areas of the Foundation Stage curriculum. (Hickson, 2005: 197–8)

Hickson's work is an example that could allay the fears expressed by Anning and Edwards (2003) that literacy in the early years continues to over-promote 'conventional' reading and writing in pre-school settings.

REFERENCES AND INDICATIVE FURTHER READING

Anning, A. and Edwards, A. (2003) 'Language and literacy learning', in J. Devereaux and L. Miller (eds), *Working with Children in the Early Years*. London: David Fulton/Open University.

Baghban, M. (1984) *Our Daughter Learns to Read and Write*. Newark, DE: International Reading Association.

Bissex, G.L. (1980) *GYNS AT WRK: A Child Learns to Write and Read*. Cambridge, MA: Harvard University Press.

Burke, C. (1982) 'Redefining written language growth: the child as informant', paper presented at the 8th Australian Reading Association Conference, Adelaide.

DES (1988) *English for Ages 5–11. Proposals of the Secretary of State for Education and Science and the Secretary of State for Wales*. London: National Curriculum Council.

DfES/QCA (2003) *Foundation Stage Profile Handbook*. London: QCA.

Ferrerio, E. and Teberosky, A. (1989) *Literacy before Schooling*. Oxford: Heinemann.

Goodman, K., Goodman, Y. and Burke, C. (1978) 'Reading for life – the psycholinguistic base', in E. Hunter-Grundin and H.U. Hunter-Grundin (eds), *Reading: Implementing the Bullock Report*. London: Ward Lock.

Goodman, Y. (1980) 'The roots of literacy', in M.P. Douglas (ed.), *Claremont Reading Conference Forty-fourth Yearbook*. Claremont, CA: Claremont Reading Association.

Goodman, Y. (1986) 'Children coming to know literacy', in W.H. Teale and E. Sulzby (eds), *Emergent Literacy Writing and Reading*. Norwood, NJ: Ablex.

Goswami, U. and Bryant, P. (1990) *Phonological Skills and Learning to Read*. Hove: Lawrence Erlbaum Associates.

Harste, J.C., Woodward, V.A. and Burke, C.L. (1984) *Language Stories and Literacy Lessons*. Portsmouth, NH: Heinemann Educational Books.

Hickson, H. (2005) 'Developing the Role of Parents in Early Writing Experiences of their Children', in C. Nutbrown, P. Hannon and A. Morgan (eds), *Early Literacy Work with Parents: Policy, Practice and Research*. London: Sage.

Hiebert, E.H. (1981) 'Developmental patterns and inter-relationships of preschool children's print awareness', *Reading Research Quarterly*, 16: 236–59.

Maclean, M., Bryant, P. and Bradley, L. (1987) 'Rhymes, nursery rhymes and reading in early childhood', *Merrill-Palmer Quarterly*, 33(3): 255–81.

Marsh, J. (ed.) (2005) *Popular Culture, New Media and Digital Literacy in Early Childhood*. London: RoutledgeFalmer.

Meek, M. (1982) *Learning to Read*. London: The Bodley Head.

Nutbrown, C. and Hannon, P. (eds) (1997) *Preparing for Early Literacy Education with Parents: A Professional Development Manual*. Sheffield/Nottingham: NES Arnold/ University of Sheffield REAL Project.

Nutbrown, C., Hannon, P. and Morgan, A. (eds) (2005) *Early Literacy Work with Parents: Policy, Practice and Research*. London: Sage.

Payton, S. (1984) *Developing Awareness of Print – a Child's First Steps Towards Literacy. Educational Review Occasional Papers No. 2*. Birmingham: University of Birmingham.

QCA (2000) *Curriculum Guidance for the Foundation Stage*. London: Qualifications and Curriculum Authority.

Ross, D.D. and Brondy, E. (1987) 'Communicating with parents about beginning reading instruction', *Childhood Education*, 63(4): 270–4.

Schickedanz, J. (1990) *Adam's Righting Revolutions*. Portsmouth, NH: Heinemann.

Smith, F. (1976) 'Learning to read by reading', *Language Arts*, 53(March): 297–9, 322.

Weinberger, J. (1996) *Literacy Goes to School – the Parents' Role in Young Children's Literacy Learning*. London: Paul Chapman Publishing.

Wells, G. (1987) *The Meaning Makers: Children Learning Language and Using Language to Learn*. London: Hodder & Stoughton.

early years foundation stage

> **The Early Years Foundation Stage is a curriculum framework to support children's learning and development from birth to five years in England.**

The establishment of the Early Years Foundation Stage (EYFS) in England began some time before it was an official requirement in 2008 and, before considering the content of the EYFS itself, its brief history is worth noting. Prior to the EYFS, which focuses on children from birth to five, the Foundation Stage for England and Wales was published in 2000 and marked an important point in recent early childhood education policy which included shifts in state funding of 'nursery' education, new regulations and regimes for inspection of under-fives provision and nationally reported assessment of four year olds in reception classes. Forerunners in the rapid policy changes included the publication of the *Desirable Outcomes for Children's Learning* (SCAA, 1996) and the *National Framework for Baseline Assessment* (SCAA, 1997) both of which met resistance from early childhood professionals and it was this challenge to policy-makers from the early childhood field that led to the development of the Foundation Stage. Four and five year olds in reception classes were no longer loosely grouped alongside pupils in Key Stage 1 but were part of the distinct phase of education focusing on children aged three to five-plus years (the end of the reception class year). This, of course, meant that some children attended a number of settings during their Foundation Stage, perhaps including a playgroup, a childminder, a nursery class and into a reception class.

For many, the introduction of the EYFS – which focused on children from birth and incorporated the earlier *Birth to Three Matters Framework* (DfES, 2002) – represented recognition at policy level of the particular learning needs of young children and built on the return of 'play' (begun in the Foundation Stage in 2000), as a key element in young children's learning. Schools and other early years providers who receive state funding for their early years provision are required to follow the EYFS and are inspected to ensure they do so. Settings where the EYFS is compulsory include reception and nursery classes in maintained and independent schools, day nurseries, playgroups, before- and after-school clubs, holiday play schemes and Sure Start/Children's Centres. The EYFS is not a requirement in parents and toddler groups, or where children are cared for by nannies or in occasional crèches. Key components are a play-based approach to learning, involvement and work with parents, information for parents on children's development and holistic approach to children's experiences taking account of their needs and abilities.

The purpose and aims of the Early Years Foundation Stage was stated thus:

1.1 Every child deserves the best possible start in life and support to fulfil their potential. A child's experience in the early years has a major impact on their future life chances. A secure, safe and happy childhood is important in its own right, and it provides the foundation for children to make the most of their abilities and talents as they grow up. When parents choose to use early years services they want to know that provision will keep their children safe and help them to thrive. The Early Years Foundation Stage (EYFS) is the framework that provides that assurance.

1.2 The overarching aim of the EYFS is to help young children achieve the five *Every Child Matters* outcomes of staying safe, being healthy, enjoying and achieving, making a positive contribution, and achieving economic well-being by:

- setting the standards for the learning, development and care young children should experience when they are attending a setting outside their family home, ensuring that every child makes progress and that no child gets left behind;
- providing for equality of opportunity and anti-discriminatory practice and ensuring that every child is included and not disadvantaged because of ethnicity, culture or religion, home language, family background, learning difficulties or disabilities, gender or ability;
- creating the framework for partnership working between parents and professionals, and between all the settings that the child attends;
- improving quality and consistency in the early years sector through a universal set of standards which apply to all settings, ending the distinction between care and learning in the existing frameworks, and providing the basis for the inspection and regulation regime;

- laying a secure foundation for future learning through learning and development that is planned around the individual needs and interests of the child, and informed by the use of ongoing observational assessment. (DCSF, 2008: 7)

The EYFS is based around four main themes:

A Unique Child – every child is a competent learner from birth who can be resilient, capable, confident and self-assured. The commitments are focused around development; inclusion; safety; and health and well-being.

Positive Relationships – children learn to be strong and independent from a base of loving and secure relationships with parents and/or a key person. The commitments are focused around respect; partnership with parents; supporting learning; and the role of the key person.

Enabling Environments – the environment plays a key role in supporting and extending children's development and learning. The commitments are focused around observation, assessment and planning; support for every child; the learning environment; and the wider context – transitions, continuity, and multi-agency working.

Learning and Development – children develop and learn in different ways and at different rates, and that all areas of learning and development are equally important and inter-connected. (DCSF, 2008: 9)

Learning and development in the EYFS comprises three elements: *early learning goals*, which set out what children should achieve by the end of the academic year in which they reach the age of five (this is problematic because some children will be just five and some will be a few months from their sixth birthday); *educational programmes*, those things which must be taught to children; and *assessment arrangements*, to check on progress during the years birth to five. The EYFS acknowledged that the six areas of learning and development described in great detail in the framework and supporting materials cannot be 'delivered' in isolation and so promotes a play-based and mixed method approach. The six areas listed in the *early learning goals and educational programmes* are:

- personal, social and emotional development;
- communication, language and literacy;
- problem-solving, reasoning and numeracy;

- knowledge and understanding of the world;
- physical development;
- creative development.

Frameworks for early learning, and inspection of settings receiving government funding were first introduced in 1989. Since then there has been a state of almost continual change. What is needed is a period of consolidation within settings and sustained professional development to enable the full range of practitioners in the early years workforce to implement and develop the framework with the professionalism that is needed. That would be in the interests of the children, respectful of their rights as capable learners, and worthy of professionals who are committed to doing the every best they can for young children.

REFERENCES AND INDICATIVE FURTHER READING

DCSF (2008) *Statutory Framework for the Early Years Foundation Stage*. Nottingham: HMSO.

DfES (2002) *Birth to Three Matters: A Framework to Support Children in their Earliest Years*. London: DfES/Sure Start.

Fisher, J. (1996) *Starting from the Child? Teaching and Learning from 4 to 8*. Buckingham: Open University Press.

Physick, R. (2005) 'Changes and challenges: preschool practitioners' responses to policy change and development', in K. Hirst and C. Nutbrown (eds), *Perspectives on Early Childhood: Essays in Contemporary Research*. Stoke-on-Trent: Trentham.

QCA (2000) *Curriculum Guidance for the Foundation Stage*. London: QCA.

SCAA (1996) *Desirable Outcomes for Children's Learning*. London: DfEE/SCAA.

SCAA (1997) *National Framework for Baseline Assessment: Criteria and procedures for the accreditation of Baseline Assessment Schemes*. London: DfEE/SCAA.

Stevens, C. (2005) 'The value of Early Years Development Officers' support for voluntary pre-school playgroups', in K. Hirst and C. Nutbrown (eds), *Perspectives on Early Childhood: Essays in Contemporary Research*. Stoke-on-Trent: Trentham.

Webster, S. (2002) 'Cinderellas in lonely castles? Perspectives of voluntary preschool supervisors in rural communities', in C. Nutbrown (ed.), *Research Studies in Early Childhood Education*. Stoke-on-Trent: Trentham.

> *Early Years Professional Status (EYPS) ensures that those working with children under the age of five benefit from the highest level of training. The skills and experience graduates acquire will not only give children brighter futures, but also enable Early Years Professionals (EYPs) to lead and inspire others to give all children the start in life they deserve. Early Years Professionals work in a wide range of roles in group settings such as nurseries and Children's Centres and as home-based childcarers. They lead practice, support other practitioners and are central to helping children develop from birth until the age of five, a crucial time in a child's life.*[5]

In a bid to develop the early childhood education and care into a graduate-led profession the Labour government, in 2007 announced its aim that there should be an Early Years Professional in every Children's Centre by 2010 and in every full day-care setting by 2015. Different routes towards gaining the status are possible, varying from a short four-month validation to a twelve-month qualification pathway. Early Years Professionals work in a range of early years settings. The Children's Workforce Development Council stated that Early Years Professionals would be 'skilled and effective' practitioners who work as part of the team in early years settings or children's services; take responsibility for leading and managing play, care and learning; and have current knowledge and understanding of early years practice with children from birth to five (CWDC, 2008). The role of the Early Years Professional is also designed to be key in leading and supporting staff in the settings in which they work on all aspects of the Early Years Foundation Stage.

The introduction of a recognised status which is named Early Years Professional raises an issue about the 'professionalism' of all staff in the early years workforce. Are not teachers, nursery nurses, those holding a range of other qualifications not also 'professional'? In fact – because they work in the early years are they not, too, early years professionals? This is an issue for the future and a matter for the wider early years

---

[5] www.cwdcouncil.org.uk/eyps/what-is-an-eyp

profession to consider. Meanwhile research into what it is to be a 'professional' in the early years, continues with views on what it is to 'care' (Swick, 2007), the heightening of 'professionalism' (Osgood, 2004), professionalism, care and business (Campbell-Barr, 2009), management and professionalism (Muijs et al., 2004) and leadership (Aubrey, 2007).

REFERENCES AND INDICATIVE FURTHER READING

Aubrey, C. (2007) *Leading and Managing in the Early Years*. London: Sage.

Campbell-Barr, V. (2009) 'Care and business orientations in the delivery of childcare: an exploratory study', *Journal of Early Childhood Research*, 7(1): 76–93.

Children's Workforce Development Council (CWDC) (2008) *Introduction and Information Guide: Early Years Professionals, Creating Brighter Futures*. Leeds: CWDC.

Muijs, D., Aubrey, C., Harris, A. and Briggs, M. (2004) 'How do they manage? A review of the research on leadership in early childhood', *Journal of Early Childhood Research*, 2(2): 157–69.

Osgood, J. (2004) 'Time to get down to business? The responses of early years practitioners to entrepreneurial approaches to professionalism', *Journal of Early Childhood Research*, 2(1): 5–24.

Swick, J.K. (2007) 'Insights on caring for early childhood professionals and families', *Early Childhood Education Journal*, 35(2): 97–102.

> ✳ *'Family Literacy' is a term used to refer to the interrelated literacy* **practices** *of parents, children and others in homes and certain kinds of educational* **programmes** *(mostly focused on disadvantaged communities) that recognise the importance of the family dimension in the literacy learning of children or parents or both.*

'Family Literacy' is a term used to refer to the interrelated literacy *practices* of parents, children and others in homes. (Barton and Hamilton, 1998; Hannon, 2000; Heath, 1983; Hirst, 1988; Taylor, 1983; Taylor and Dorsey-Gaines, 1988; Teale, 1986; Weinberger, 1996). The term also refers to certain kinds of educational *programmes* (mostly focused on disadvantaged communities) that recognise the importance of the family dimension in the literacy learning of children or parents or both (Cairney and Munsie, 1995; Dickinson, 1994; Hannon, 1995; Hannon and Nutbrown, 1997; Morrow, 1995; Wolfendale and Topping, 1996).

Family Literacy research has become indispensable for a full understanding of how young children learn literacy and how they may be taught or helped to acquire it. Family Literacy programmes belong to the field of adult learning as well as to early childhood education but for the purposes of this volume which is concerned with early childhood literacy, programmes are viewed mainly from the perspective of early childhood education.

Hannon summarises:

Within the early childhood education strand, parental involvement in the teaching of literacy began, after a long period of routine parental exclusion, with a focus on parents helping children's oral reading. It has gradually evolved to take on a broader concept of literacy, preschool as well as school-aged children, and support for a wider range of at-home as well as in-school activities. These actions by schools can be counted as family literacy programmes in that they clearly 'acknowledge and make use of learners' family relationships' but it must be admitted that the learners with which they are concerned are mainly young children and that on the whole programmes have not so much been concerned with 'engagement in family literacy practices' as families' engagement in school literacy practices. (Hannon, 2004: 97)

Research into Family Literacy practices and programmes has, over the past two decades, involved three main approaches: observing and recording literacy practices in the home (Bissex, 1980; Clay, 1975; Nutbrown, 1999; Schickedanz, 1990; Tizard and Hughes, 1984); soliciting views and reports from parents, (Hannon and James, 1990; Hirst, 1998; Parker, 1986; Weinberger, 1996) and children (Nutbrown and Hannon, 2003); evaluating learning outcomes for children and adults (Brooks et al., 1996, 1997; Edwards, 1994; Tizard et al., 1982; Whitehurst et al., 1994).

Hannon (2000) identifies seven key research issues: deficit approaches, targeting of programmes, evidence of effectiveness, gender, bilingualism, training for practitioners and policy research. While some of these have attracted considerable research interest and activity; others remain under-researched.

In the United States many Family Literacy programmes have been developed and delivered by agencies whose mission was primarily to do with adults, including libraries, colleges, adult education services, prison organisations, services to users of day care or Head Start. In England, the Adult Literacy and Basic Skills Unit promoted government-funded 'family literacy' promoting a largely US model aimed at parents' as well as children's literacy.

THE RAISING EARLY ACHIEVEMENT IN LITERACY (REAL) PROJECT

The REAL Family Literacy programme, developed and implemented by teachers at 11 schools, was 'long duration' (18 months) and 'low intensity'. It was based on a conceptual ORIM framework developed by Hannon and Nutbrown (1997) in which parents are seen as providing opportunities, recognition, interaction and a model of literacy. The programme framework and examples of activities are fully reported (Nutbrown and Hannon, 1997; Nutbrown et al., 2005) and included five components:

- home visits by programme teachers;
- provision of literacy resources;
- centre-based group activities;
- special events;
- postal communication.

In these ways the programme sought to promote children's experience with family members of four strands of early literacy development: writing, reading and rhyming at home and greater awareness of environmental print. There was also an optional adult education component where parents were given information about local adult education classes and the opportunity to develop a portfolio of the work they had done with their child for accreditation. Details of the ORIM framework (see 104–6) and programme evaluation, including literacy outcomes for children, are given in Nutbrown et al. (2005).

REFERENCES AND INDICATIVE FURTHER READING

Barton, D. and Hamilton, M. (1998) *Local Literacies: Reading and Reading in One Community*. London: Routledge.

Bissex, G. (1980) *GYNS AT WRK: A Child Learns to Write and Read*. Cambridge, MA: Harvard University Press.

Brooks, G., Gorman, T., Harman, D. and Wilkin, A. (1996) *Family Literacy Works: The NFER Evaluation of the Basic Skills Agency's Family Literacy Demonstration Programmes*. London: Basic Skills Agency.

Brooks, G., Gorman, T., Harman, J., Hutchison, D., Kinder, K., Moor, H. and Wilkin, A. (1997) *Family Literacy Lasts: The NFER Follow-up Study of the Basic Skills Agency's Demonstration Programmes*. London: Basic Skills Agency.

Cairney, T.H. and Munsie, L. (1995) *Beyond Tokenism: Parents as Partners in Literacy*. Portsmouth, NH: Heinemann.

Clay, M.M. (1975) *What Did I Write?* Auckland, NZ: Heinemann Educational.

Dickinson, D. (ed.) (1994) *Bridges to Literacy: Children, Families and Schools*. Oxford: Blackwell.

Edwards, P.A. (1994) 'Responses of teachers and African-American mothers to a book-reading intervention program', in D. Dickinson (ed.), *Bridges to Literacy: Children, Families and Schools*. Oxford: Blackwell.

Hannon, P. (1995) *Literacy, Home and School: Research and Practice in Teaching Literacy with Parents*. London: Falmer Press.

Hannon, P. (2000) 'Rhetoric and research in family literacy', *British Educational Research Journal*, 26(1): 121–38.

Hannon, P. (2004) 'The development of family literacy in early childhood education', in N. Hall, J. Lorson and J. Marsh (eds), *Handbook of Early Childhood Literacy Research*. London: Sage.

Hannon, P. and James, S. (1990) 'Parents' and teachers' perspectives on preschool literacy development', *British Educational Research Journal*, 16(3): 259–72.

Hannon, P. and Nutbrown, C. (1997) 'Teachers' use of conceptual framework for early literacy education involving parents', *Teacher Development*, 1(3): 405–20.

Hannon, P. and Nutbrown, C. (2001) 'Outcomes for children and parents of an early literacy education parental involvement programme', paper presented at the Annual Conference of the British Educational Research Association, Leeds.

family literacy

Harrison, C. (1996) 'Family literacy: evaluation, ownership and ambiguity', *Royal Society of Arts Journal*, November: 1–4.

Heath, S.B. (1983) *Ways With Words: Language, Life and Work in Communities and Classrooms.* Cambridge: Cambridge University Press.

Hirst, K. (1998) 'Pre-school literacy experiences of children in Punjabi, Urdu and Gujerati speaking families in England', *British Educational Research Journal*, 24(4): 415–29.

Morrow, L.M. (ed.) (1995) *Family Literacy: Connections in Schools and Communities.* Newark, DE: International Reading Association.

Nutbrown, C. (1999) 'Learning about literacy in the earliest years: Alex's story', in E. Millard (ed.), *Enquiries into Literacy.* Sheffield: University of Sheffield Papers in Education.

Nutbrown, C. and Hannon, P. (eds) (1997) *Preparing for Early Literacy Work with Families: A Professional Development Manual.* Nottingham/Sheffield: NES Arnold/ REAL Project.

Nutbrown, C. and Hannon, P. (2003) 'Children's perspectives on early literacy: issues and methodologies', *Journal of Early Childhood Literacy*, 3(2): 115–45.

Nutbrown, C., Hannon, P. and Morgan, A. (2005) *Early Literacy Work with Families: Policy, Practice and Research.* London: Sage.

Parker, S. (1986) '"I want to give them what I never had" Can parents who are barely literate teach their children to read?', *Times Educational Supplement*, 10 October: 23.

Schickedanz, J. (1990) *Adam's Righting Revolutions.* Portsmouth, NH: Heinemann.

Taylor, D. (1983) *Family Literacy: Young Children Learning to Read and Write.* Exeter, NH: Heinemann.

Taylor, D. and Dorsey-Gaines, C. (1988) *Growing up Literate: Learning from inner-city Families.* Portsmouth, NH: Heinemann.

Teale, W.H. (1986) 'Home background and young children's literacy development', in W.H. Teale and E. Sulzby (eds), *Emergent Literacy: Writing and Reading*, Norwood, NJ: Ablex. pp. 173–206.

Tizard, B. and Hughes, M. (1984) *Young Children Learning: Talking and Thinking at Home and in School.* London: Falmer.

Tizard, J., Schofield, W.N. and Hewison, J. (1982) 'Collaboration between teachers and parents in assisting children's reading', *British Journal of Educational Psychology*, 52: 1–15.

Weinberger, J. (1996) *Literacy Goes to School: the Parents' Role in Young Children's Literacy Learning.* London: Paul Chapman Publishing.

Whitehurst, G.J., Epstein, J.N., Angell, A.L., Payne, D.A., Crone D.A. and Fischel, J.E. (1994) 'Outcomes of an emergent literacy intervention Head Start', *Journal of Educational Pyschology*, 86(4): 542–55.

Wolfendale, S. and Topping, K. (eds) (1996) *Family Involvement in Literacy: Effective Partnerships in Education.* London: Cassell.

gender

Gender influences and stereotyping in children's play in early years settings is a much studied topic. Gender identities, what it is to be a boy or
a girl, are a strong feature of children's play and often impact on their
choices of types of play and 'playmates'.

Several studies have explored issues of gender in children's play in the
early years (Davies, 1989; MacNaughton, 1999; Tarullo, 1994), and gender identity is a strong feature in young children's lives. Much has been
written about 'sexual equality' and gender divides in society, and interest
in implications and effects of gender on young children's learning and
experiences is rooted in a tradition of studies which have sought to
understand, and later challenge, stereotypes and limited opportunities.

Tarullo (1994) suggested that girls and boys speak with 'different
voices' in their experiences of the world and there is broad agreement
in the literature that boys and girls show different kinds of behaviour
and preferences in their play (Maccoby and Jacklin, 1974; Gussin Paley,
1984). Where girls and boys do share the same play area they have often
been found to use it differently, for example:

> The play area of playhouse is a largely female domain and children often
> assume stereotypical roles on entering it. Girls are pleased to act out stories
> and situations. However, boys seem unhappy in deferring to the girls in
> the context and I have often observed boys changing roles to become
> animals, introducing elements of aggression, noise and disruption to the
> situation. (D'Arcy, 1990: 84)

Clear preferences are often exhibited, perhaps because this is one way
in which children create and begin to identify with their own gender. As
MacNaughton suggests:

> Children's pretend play is rich in information about how they understand
> gender relations. As children play at 'having babies', 'being monsters', or
> 'making a hospital', children show others what they think girls and women
> can and should do, and what they think boys and men can and should do.
> (MacNaughton, 1999: 81)

gender

There are many issues which arise from the study of gender in early childhood education which in turn give rise to the need for further detailed study. Further understanding of this theme requires a focus on: professional development for practitioners; understanding the influence of parents and children's out-of-school/care lives; how children demonstrate what they know about men and women – and girls and boys – through their own gendered play; and the impact of gendered play on learning choices and achievements.

Professional development of educators in terms of gender and gendered practices is an important area of study. Examination of play and gendered influences and outcomes of children's play can help to challenge gendered choices by children which may limit children's access to particular areas of learning and avenues of understanding. For example, MacNaughton's (2000) study involving teachers demonstrated that many teaching practices and strategies, and provision for free play, influenced the development of children's gendered identities. In her study, boys and girls consistently preferred different areas of provision and demonstrated ways of dominating the areas they chose. Through a programme of professional development the teachers adjusted their practices and were able to identify and implement a range of pedagogical practices which enabled the gendered responses of children to the provision they used to be reviewed, challenged and changed. Connolly's work on boys and schooling in the early years (2004) examines young boys and achievement and argues that the lower educational performance of boys in the early years must be addressed. Connolly argues that there is a need to work within what he calls the 'Critical Gender Zone' which he defines as: 'the distance between what a child has already come to internalise in terms of their current experiences of gender relations and the degree to which they are able to reflect upon and deconstruct these with the help of others' (Connolly, 2004: 229–30).

The role of parents and children's home and families in influencing their 'out of setting' lives is an area which would benefit from further study. Though many studies have been developed on children's gendered identities, in the context of the twenty-first century it is important fully to understand the impact of social and cultural influences on children's constructions of their gender identities. Three studies by teachers (Leslie, 2005; Tacey, 2005; Walters, 2002) examine the impact of families and parents on children's preferences for particular toys and of the construction of their gendered identities. Walters', (2002) study involving parents of ten four-year-old children (five boys and five girls) showed that parents had clear ideas about the appropriateness of toys for girls and boys, and the boys liked cars, trucks and construction toys while girls preferred soft toys, Barbie dolls and dressing up games. Walters found a stereotypical view of girls' and boys' toys which led her to reflect on the implications for children's learning and all round development. Tacey (2005), however, in a similar study found that some parents were actively promoting non-stereotypical choices of toys at home and believed that the school promoted the development of narrow stereotypes of gendered identity.

Vivian Gussin Paley reminds us that combating stereotypical behaviours of young children is not easy:

> Kindergarten is a triumph of sexual stereotyping. No amount of adult subterfuge or propaganda deflects the five year old's passion for segregation by sex. They think they have invented the differences between boys and girls and, as with any new invention, must prove that it works. The doll corner is often the best place to collect evidence. It is not simply a place to play; it is a stronghold against ambiguity. (Gussin Paley, 1984: ix)

HOMES AND COMPUTERS

In a nursery class the teacher noticed that the girls tended always to dominate the home corner area and the boys the computer area. When she talked to the children they told her that they chose these things because the home area was 'for girls' and the computers were 'for boys'. She challenged their thinking asking who lived and did domestic chores at home and who used the family computer. The children's answers showed that stereotypical behaviour they displayed in the nursery was not reflecting their home lives. They had mothers who used computers and fathers who washed up. This example represents many research studies which have shown that young children often gravitate to stereotypical aspects of provision often defying (or denying) the experience in their daily lives. The teacher concluded that stereotypes could only be challenged through ongoing and deliberate intervention strategies which broadened out opportunities for children.

'GIRLS ONLY' COMPUTER ZONE

In a playgroup setting the boys dominated the only computer, refusing to allow girls an opportunity to use the games. This continued for several sessions and practitioners discussed fairness, sharing and taking turns to no avail. Finally it was decided that the staff should declare the computer area a 'girls only zone' until further notice. This brought incessant complaints about injustices and unfairness from the indignant boys who were clearly shocked by the decision to ban them from their favourite activity. It did, however, make it possible for staff to demonstrate that equipment should be shared and eventually a turn-taking system was established – often successful when policed by staff or when girls reported a breach of the rules.

In both of the above examples all the members of staff were female, and in each case they felt that the lack of male role models in the settings made it more difficult to address gender issues through modelling both sexes working in all areas of the provision. The women also felt that they tended to avoid some areas – particularly large construction bricks – and concluded that they needed to examine the messages they gave to children about 'what women do'.

In a project designed to develop strategies to allow boys more access to home-corner play the children were first asked for their views. One five-year-old girl said:

> I like 'baby born' best; I like the black dolly. Wish we could have Barbies at nursery, we like Barbies but nursery 'an't got 'ny and the bits get lost if you bring your own so I don't.

Another expressed the view that:

> The boys can't come in here 'cos they make a noise and they mess it up, and they act like dogs and angry husbands.

A third said:

> Sometimes I put the ironing board across the doorway so the boys can't get in … 'cos there's no door and you need one. (Nutbrown and Clough, 2009: 201–2)

The teacher and other staff developed a number of strategies and, as well as maintaining the usual home play space, staff included other role-play areas which they chose in consultation with the children. Over time they established a garage, a tropical fish shop, a hairdressing salon, a chip shop and an office (familiar practice in many settings, but new to this one). Several of these new opportunities gave rise to fewer instances of gender-dominated play and created spaces for boys to engage in more positive role-play activities which were not dominated and controlled by the girls. Practitioners in this setting continued to help boys negotiate their way 'past the ironing board' into the home corner which often remains a mainly female domain.

REFERENCES AND INDICATIVE FURTHER READING

Blaise, M. and Andrew, Y. (2005) 'How "bad" can it be? Troubling gender, sexuality and early childhood teaching', in N. Yelland (ed.) *Critical Issues in Early Childhood Education*. Buckingham: Open University Press.

Cameron, C., Moss, P. and Owen, C. (1999) *Men in the Nursery: Gender and Caring Work*. London: Paul Chapman Publishing.

Connolly, P. (2004) *Boys and Schooling in the Early Years*. London: RoutledgeFalmer.

D'Arcy, S. (1990) 'Towards a non-sexist primary classroom', in E. Tutchell (ed.), *Dolls and Dungarees: Gender Issues in the Primary School Curriculum*. Milton Keynes: Open University Press.

Davies, B. (1989) *Frogs, Snails and Feminist Tales*. Sydney: George Allen & Unwin.

Gussin Paley, V. (1984) *Boys and Girls: Superheroes in the Doll Corner*. Chicago, IL and London: University of Chicago Press.

Leslie, R. (2005) 'Seeing gender through young girls' eyes', in K. Hirst and C. Nutbrown (eds), *Perspectives on Early Childhood Education: Essays in Contemporary Research*. Stoke-on Trent: Trentham.

Maccoby, E.E. and Jacklin, C.N. (1974) *The Psychology of Sex Differences*. Vol. 1. Stanford, CA: Stanford University Press.

MacNaughton, G. (1999) 'Even pink tents have glass ceilings: crossing the gender boundaries in pretend play', in E. Dau and E. Jones (eds), *Child's Play: Revisiting Play in Early Childhood Settings*. Sydney: MacLennan & Petty Pty Ltd.

MacNaughton, G. (2000) *Rethinking Gender in Early Childhood Education*. New York: Sage.

Nutbrown, C. and Clough, P (2009) 'Citizenship and inclusion in the early years: understanding and responding to children's perspectives on "belonging"', *International Journal of Early Years Education*, 17(3): 191–205.

Tacey, C. (2005) 'Why do boys like to build and girls like to draw? Gender issues in a small British military community', in K. Hirst and C. Nutbrown (eds), *Perspectives on Early Childhood Education: Essays in Contemporary Research*. Stoke-on Trent: Trentham.

Tarullo, L.B. (1994) 'Windows on social worlds: gender differences in children's play narratives', in A. Slade and P.D. Wolf (eds), *Children at Play: Clinical and Developmental Approaches to Meaning and Representation*. New York: Oxford University Press.

Walters, N. (2002) 'Gender roles and toys in the home: parents' attitudes and children's experiences', in C. Nutbrown (ed.), *Research Studies in Early Childhood Education*. Stoke-on Trent: Trentham.

Yelland, N. (ed.) (1998) *Gender in Early Childhood Education*. London: Routledge.

gender

heuristic play with objects

Heuristic play with objects is an approach to working with children in their second year of life – when they are at 'toddler' stage. This 'method' was developed and practised by Elinor Goldschmied working with practitioners in England, Scotland, Italy and Spain.

Heuristic play is seen as a specific approach which is offered to children as part of daily provision alongside other rich and varied experiences. An understanding of the term and its origins provides an important underpinning to appreciating the purpose of this approach with young children.

The word 'heuristic' derives from the Greek 'eurisko' which means 'serves to discover' or 'gain an understanding of … ' which describes exactly what these children are engaged in. By introducing this unusual word attention is focussed, in a respectful way, on the quality and dignity of what these children do, spontaneously, if provided with appropriate materials, by themselves and for themselves without active adult intervention.(Goldschmied and Hughes, 1992)

Goldschmied and Jackson (2003:118) summarise the practice of Heuristic play thus: 'Put simply it consists of offering a group of children, for a defined period of time in a controlled environment, a large number of different kinds of objects and receptacles with which they play freely without adult intervention.'

Key sources for understanding the underlying principles and practices of heuristic play are Goldschmied and Jackson (2003) and Goldschmied and Hughes (1992). Heuristic play offers young children who are 'on the move' the opportunity to explore what they can do with a range of objects and how those objects behave. The adult's role is very much affirming the child's play as he/she is problem-solving, sorting, balancing, filling, and so on. A practitioner may need to intervene if there is conflict (though Goldschmied argues that if there are sufficient quantities of everything conflict over materials rarely arises) and can offer simple vocabulary such as 'it is by Melissa' or 'look underneath your hand'. The heuristic play session offers a good opportunity to observe children's behaviour. It is imperative that all practitioners and parents are familiar with reasons for offering such provision for young children within the day so that the uses and benefits to children's learning and development can be maximised.

Heuristic play is part of work with children under three years of age. Heuristic play sessions have been used in many settings to support young children's exploration and learning. There are a number of research issues which arise from these practices, and further study could enhance our understanding of the following:

- What are the roles of the adults during heuristic play sessions?
- How do practitioners who play the active, almost silent, and supportive observer make decisions about their role?
- What are the children doing?
- How is their learning being extended and in what ways does their activity in heuristic play sessions connect with the very different provision that they may be offered during other parts of their day?

Given that parents are key to young children's holistic learning and development, more work could be done on how the purposes and practices of heuristic play sessions are communicated to parents and how parents are helped to view their own role in providing for the exploration of objects in a home setting.

Young children, given the choice of a range of materials, can focus, for some time on exploring what they can do with objects that interest them. The following examples show how the heuristic play space is set out by the adult and used by the children and finally tidied away.

In a pleasant, carpeted room, Mary began to set out the objects in readiness for the heuristic play session. To avoid children getting into tussles over a particular object, she ensured that there was plenty of everything: metal tins, balls, cockle shells, lengths of ribbon in different colours and textures, cardboard tubes of different lengths, wooden and metal curtain rings, pine cones. She selected some calming music and started it playing softly. She checked around the room to ensure that objects were well spaced and attractively presented, and positioned the low comfortable chair for her to sit unobtrusively while she watched the children. She left to collect the children.

Jamie (14 months) had chosen a large metal tin and placed it on the floor near the watching adult. He wandered around the space and returned with a length of red velvet ribbon which he had chosen. He placed it in the tin. He pulled it out, put it in, pulled it out and finally placed it carefully in the tin. He walked around the room again and returned with a large wooden curtain ring which he fingered and turned in his small hand. He placed it in the tin, looked at it – lying against the red velvet ribbon. He removed the curtain ring, then placed it in the tin again. Jamie made several trips around the room each time returning with a different object: a shell, a cardboard tube, a pine cone.

Nikki (17 months) found a large cardboard tube. She walked around the room carrying and waving the tube. She looked through it. She turned the tube and looked through from the other end. She dropped the tube and picked up another tube, smaller than the first, she looked through it, turned it and looked through the other end. Nikki worked her way around the room, looking through several tubes and then seemingly abandoning them where she found them. She picked up a large shiny metal tin and held it to her face, looking through it in the same way – this time she saw the reflection of her own face in the bottom of the tin. She giggled.

Among a number of children who were using their recently acquired mobility to find objects which attracted their interest from different parts of the room sat Simone (13 months). Simone was quite a good walker, having taken her first steps at 11 months, but today she was sitting – absorbed in her exploration of a brass chain (about 20 centimetres long – each link about 5 millimetres in length). Slowly and carefully, and with great attention (seemingly unaware of the other children moving around her – one making quite a noise by dropping shells into a tin) Simone watched the chain as she lowered it to the floor. She raised her arm again, watching the chain unfurl and become straight again as she held it up. She explored the fluidity of the chain for quite a time – repeating the up and down movement of her arm. Her face showed a slight frown – such was her concentration.

At end of the session Mary involved all the children in helping tidy up. The room looked somewhat dishevelled with tubes, ribbons, tins, shells, and so on seemingly scattered everywhere. Mary began by modelling how to collect each type of object into its own bag. She walked around the room collecting tins first and asking children – using clear simple language – to help in the process. Next Mary opened a large bag and gestured to the children to put all the cardboard tubes inside. Next a bag was filled with shells, another with curtain rings and so on until the room was cleared and all the objects were in their bags which Mary then placed on hooks in a store room. The children seemed to enjoy this 'filling the bag' activity – for many it appealed to their interest in enclosing (see schemas, p. 133).

REFERENCES AND INDICATIVE FURTHER READING

Gillespie Edwards, A. (2002) *Relationships and Learning: Caring for Children from Birth to Three.* London: NCB

Goldschmied, E. and Jackson, S. (2003) *People Under Three: Young Children in Day Care.* London: Routledge. (Chapter 8 'Heuristic play with objects' gives examples of children's play during heuristic play sessions and offers guidelines for setting up sessions and suggestions of types and quantities of objects to be used in heuristic play.)

Goldschmied, E. and Hughes, A. (1992) *Heuristic Play with Objects: Children of 12–20 Months Exploring Everyday Objects.* London: National Children's Bureau. (DVD)

Lindon, J. (2000) *Helping Babies and Toddlers Learn: A Guide to Good Practice with Under-threes.* London: NCB.

Page, J. (2005) 'Working with the under threes', in K. Hirst and C. Nutbrown (eds), *Perspectives on Early Childhood Education: Essays in Contemporary Research.* Stoke-on-Trent: Trentham.

heuristic play with objects

high scope preschool curriculum

> **The High Scope Preschool Curriculum is a well-known approach to early learning which views children as active participants in their learning, modelled on Piagetian learning theories.**

The High Scope Preschool Curriculum has its origins in an early intervention programme carried out in the United States in the 1960s. Developed in Ypsilanti, Michigan, the High Scope approach is widely used in many countries in the world. The curriculum is planned within a clear framework which informs classroom design, and teacher intervention which ensures that children are active participants in their own learning. It is intended to be suitable for children with and without learning difficulties and physical impairment. Central to the High Scope Preschool Curriculum is the 'plan–do–review' model within which each child is encouraged to *plan* how to use their time and the resources available, *do* what they planned and 'finally' to *review* their work by discussing it with other children and their teacher. A key role for the teacher is to support children as they make their decisions and to help them carry out their work and ensure that they develop a broad repertoire of experience (and do not always choose the same tasks), and encourage skills of expression in the reviewing and reporting of their activities. Important features of the High Scope Preschool Curriculum include:

Active learning – using many direct experiences designed to support children's cognitive, physical, social and emotional development.
Adult–child interaction – allowing children to follow their chosen activities in the company of teachers who use observation and appropriate levels of involvement to enhance and extend children's thinking, cooperation, decision-making and problem-solving.
Learning environment – organised so that areas are clearly defined and labelled, often using symbols which allow the children easily to identify them. The design of the environment is intended to maximise children's independent access to learning areas and equipment.

Routine – the daily, 'plan–do–review' routine becomes familiar to the children and is a system which gives children choices in relation to their learning experiences, both indoors and outdoors and in small and larger groups.

Assessment – is carried out mainly through observation using a High Scope Child Observation Record (suitable for children aged two-and-a-half to six years). Observations of children are used to plan further experiences and to share with parents.

The High Scope Preschool Curriculum identifies 58 'key experiences' in which children should engage. These experiences are grouped into ten clusters which, together, create a broad, balanced and developmentally appropriate curriculum. They are:

- creative representation;
- language and literacy;
- initiative and social relations;
- movement;
- music;
- classification;
- seriation;
- number;
- space;
- time.

A key research issue for any specific approach to teaching and learning revolves around its effectiveness in promoting children's learning. Longitudinal evaluations of programmes using the High Scope approach have demonstrated positive developmental outcomes and sustained benefits in adulthood, such as improved social responsibility, lower rates of delinquency and later socio-economic success.

A recent study, part of the widely recognised High Scope Perry Preschool Project, included interviews of 97 per cent of study participants who were interviewed when they reached the age of 40 years. These adults attended a High Scope Preschool Programme when they were three and four years old. Study participants were African Americans who were born in poverty and at risk of dropping out of school. Control group members were also interviewed (they had not attended a High Scope Preschool Programme). The study found that, at age 40, the adults who had attended the preschool programme had higher earnings, were more likely to be in employment, had committed fewer crimes and were more likely to have graduated from high school than the adults who had not attended the High Scope Preschool Programme. The full study is reported in Schweinhart et al. (2004).

Research issues for settings using a High Scope approach to the curriculum focus on how children can be supported as active learners and ways in which particular forms of adult intervention can enhance learning.

The following example demonstrates how a High Scope approach can be adapted in a pre-school nursery setting:

In a nursery class in the North of England, a group of children gather with their key practitioner to choose their morning tasks. The children each select, from a range of magnetic symbols, three which represent the 'jobs' they will do that morning. Sally chooses a paint pot which means she plans to paint first, and places it next to her name on a large board. Next to it she attaches a picture of a book, she intends to go to the book corner after she has painted. Finally, she places a picture of a doll on the board. She intends to end her morning playing in the dolly corner. She tells the teacher:'These are my jobs – painting, reading and then playing with the dollies – I might put them in a pram and take them outside.'

Sally and the other children go about their selected 'jobs' for much of the morning. After she has painted, Sally returns to the 'jobs board' to check what she was planning to do next – she had forgotten and told her teacher: 'I couldn't think what I put so I'm checking what's next.'

At the end of the morning, the children gather in their groups with their key practitioner. They hold a 'meeting' and each shares something about their work that morning, Some show a painting, some give a verbal account of their play, one child points over to the brick corner where an elaborate construction remains. In this way the children are involved in reviewing their morning and showing responsibility for carrying out the activities they selected.

High Scope Ireland encompasses providers in voluntary, statutory, independent and community sectors in Northern Ireland and the Republic of Ireland. Emphasis is placed on the participation of parents and children with practitioners to empower children and their families and thus enhance development and enable young children and their parents to develop their potential as citizens. The High Scope Preschool Programmes are seen, in High Scope Ireland as a means of combating social disadvantage and promoting social inclusion in highly disadvantaged communities throughout Ireland. An extensive and accessible training programme is offered to promote appropriate practice and development. A Cross Border High Scope project, commissioned by the European Union (EU) Programme for Peace and Reconciliation, was developed in 2005 with the aim of enhancing the quality of early childhood provision. This is an example of using pre-school programmes as a way of investing in future positive development of communities.

REFERENCES AND INDICATIVE FURTHER READING

Barnett, W.S. (1996) *Lives in the Balance: Age 27 Benefit–cost Analysis of the High Scope Perry Preschool Program.* Monograph of the High Scope Educational Research Foundation, N.11. Ypsilanti, MI: High Scope Press.

Epstein, A. (1998) 'Is the High Scope educational approach compatible with the revised Head Start performance standards? Yes!', *High Scope Resource*, 17(2): 8–11.

Schweinhart, L.J. and Weikart, D.P. (1993a) *A Summary of the Significant Benefits: The High Scope Perry Preschool Study Through Age 27.* Yipsilanti, MI: High Scope Press.

Schweinhart, L.J. and Weikart, D.P. (1993b) 'Success by empowerment: the High Scope Perry Preschool Study through age 27', *Young Children*, 49(1): 54–8.

Schweinhart, L.J., Barnes, H.V. and Weikart, D.P. (1993) *Significant Benefits: The High Scope Perry Preschool Study Through Age 27.* Monograph of the High Scope Educational Research Foundation, N. 10. Ypsilanti, MI: High Scope Press.

Schweinhart, L.J., Montie, J., Xiang, Z., Barnett, W.S., Belfield, C.R. and Nores, M. (2004) *Lifetime Effects: The High Scope Perry Preschool Study Through Age 40.* Monograph of the High Scope Educational Research Foundation. Ypsilanti, MI: High Scope Press.

Schweinhart, L.J., Weikart, D.P. and Larner, M. (1986) 'Consequences of three pre-school curriculum models through age 15', *Early Childhood Research Quarterly*, 4(2): 97–106.

Definitions of the term 'Inclusion' are contested. However, at its broadest, inclusion in relation to early childhood education and care refers to the values, practices and attitudes around the creating communities of learning which involve and 'belong to' all members of that community: pupils, parents, staff and others connected with the setting in some way.

The term 'inclusive education' has itself come to mean many different things, which can in itself create confusion for students in this area. It is, in fact, a contestable term used to different effect by politicians, bureaucrats and academics. '"Inclusion" is not a single *movement*; it is made up of many strong currents of belief, many different local struggles and a myriad forms of practices'. (Clough and Corbett, 2000: 6)

In the UK of the twenty-first century there is increasing demand for inclusive practices and equality of opportunity and access to educational provision. But this has not always been the case, and the origins of inclusive education lie in a history of exclusion, segregation and inequality.

Clough (2000) traced the roots of Inclusion through the last half of the twentieth century (Figure 3) from the psycho-medical legacy of the 1950s through the sociological response of the 1960s, curricular approaches which dominated the 1970s, school improvement strategies and programmes of the 1980s, to the disability studies critique and the challenge by the disability movement to the state education system of the 1990s. While acknowledging that this perspective is not the only way of viewing historical developments, Clough suggests that it is these different 'eras' and developments which have led to the current 'era' of Inclusion.

It is perhaps because of such roots that 'inclusive education' is sometimes viewed as the latest term to describe the education of children with special educational needs in mainstream education settings. However, this is not how advocates of inclusive education (or of a broader social inclusion) necessarily define the term. As Booth has it:

> Some continue to want to make inclusion primarily about 'special needs education' or the inclusion in education of children and young people with

1950s ↓	The Psycho-Medical Legacy					
1960s ↓		The Sociological Response				
1970s ↓			Curricular Approaches			
1980s ↓				School Improvement Strategies		
1990s ↓					Disability Studies Critique	
2000s ↓						Inclusive Education

Figure 3 *An historical interpretation of the development and interaction of ideologies leading to present thinking in inclusive education (Adapted from Clough, 2009: 9)*

impairments but that position seems absurd … If inclusion is about the development of comprehensive community education and about prioritising community over individualism beyond education, then the history of inclusion is the history of these struggles for an education system which serves the interests of communities and which does not exclude anyone within those communities. (Booth, 2000: 64)

As provision for education and care for children of all ages considers ways of meeting education targets together with wider social challenges, the 'broad' view of Inclusion seems to be gaining currency. Lingard (2000: 101) similarly emphasises the larger structures of Inclusion in diversity: 'What I want to do is to hold to a broader definition which links across the whole social justice, equity and citizenship issues. The concept of inclusion might also encourage an across-government approach to social and economic disadvantage.'

Barton has argued a major role for inclusive practices in education in order to realise wider changes in society:

Inclusion is a process. Inclusive education is not merely about providing access into mainstream school for pupils who have previously been excluded. It is not about closing down an unacceptable system of segregated provision and dumping those pupils in an unchanged mainstream system. Existing school systems – in terms of physical factors, curriculum aspects, teaching expectations and styles, leadership roles – will have to change. This is because inclusive education is about the participation of all children and young people and the removal of all forms of exclusionary practice. (Barton, 1998: 85)

The development of inclusive education raises many research issues including:

- the practicalities of fully inclusive education;
- conflicting understandings and definitions of what is meant by 'Inclusion';
- the impact of Inclusion and exclusion on the lives of young children;
- parents views and responses to the Inclusion and/or exclusion of their children.

Some argue that children with particular needs are difficult to include in mainstream settings and attempts to include children who experience, for example, emotional and behavioural difficulties, can be detrimental to some children unless managed with the utmost knowledge and skill (Angelides, 2000; Clough, et al., 2004; Visser et al., 2003). Others take the view that there is no justification for the segregation of children in 'Special Schools' because they have a particular impairment (Herbert 1998). Further research is needed to understand the relationship between Inclusion and Special Educational Needs and between Inclusion and other issues of social justice. Mairian Corker put it this way:

I don't like using the term 'special needs' – it's paradoxical to 'inclusion'. I worry that it is increasingly part of a labelling process that is used to pick children off or as a justification for a lack of or a redistribution of resources in a way that is not in the child's interests. These labels are very dehumanising – they really get to the nub of why we are disabled people and not people with disabilities. (Corker, 2000: 77)

As Booth (2000) and Lingard (2000) illustrate, definitions of inclusion are contestable what is meant by 'Inclusion' varies from culture to culture, society to society, institution to institution and individual to individual. For example, in some parts of the world (perhaps particularly in the southern hemisphere) the Inclusion of indigenous children in education is a key issue in terms of education and social policy and for research (Fleer and Williams-Kennedy, 2001). In other parts of the world inclusion of refugee and asylum-seeking families is an issue. Some Travelling families find that they are excluded from educational services or that attempts to include them threaten to violate their cultural heritage and ways of living (Lloyd et al., 2003).

The impact of Inclusion and exclusion on the lives of young children is a further area for study; we need to know more about the human impact of decisions about young children's early education and care, and how pedagogy and learning communities affect their lives and well-being. Parents' views and responses to the Inclusion and/or exclusion of their children is a further critical area for research. Berry's study of four young children's experiences of Inclusion (Berry, 2002) demonstrates how important it is that parents have their say in the education of the children they know best and Murray uses poetry and narrative to give voice to parents' experiences of fighting for Inclusion as a right for their children (Murray and Penman, 1996).

Inclusive education is as much about helping children to behave inclusively as it is about including particularly marginalised groups of society. Gussin Paley's work (1992) provides one profound example of pedagogy which helps children to include everyone in their play; Gussin Paley's well-known book *You Can't Say You Can't Play* (1992) documents the development and agreement of this 'rule' for the kindergarten which led to complex understandings and negotiations within an emotionally supportive setting. Gussin Paley's work is not specifically about children with impairment or a particular identified need, but focuses on helping children voice their own stories and demonstrates her pedagogy of inclusion of all children's contributions in the learning setting. Addressing unfairness and discrimination is recorded by Babette Brown in her book *Unlearning Discrimination in the Early Years* (Brown, 1998) describes how children were supported by their parents and teachers to challenge discrimination and bias:

> Children can become active, enthusiastic and independent learners if, as their educators, we value their cultures and communities, and understand how racism and other social inequalities influence their lives. With our guidance and support children can, as this example illustrates, actively challenge unfairness:

A group of 6 year old children were looking through a toy catalogue. They told their teacher that they thought that it wasn't fair because there were no pictures of black children or any showing girls building or climbing. It was agreed that they should write a letter to the manufacturer. They got no reply so they wrote again. This letter was also unacknowledged. The disappointed children enthusiastically agreed with a parent who suggested that they should draw up a petition. Children, staff and parents signed and it was sent off. To the children's delight the company replied that in future pictures in the catalogue would be more carefully chosen. (Brown, 1998: 3)

The above example shows how children can, with support, challenge exclusive practices and learn strategies to argue for social justice.

WORKING WITH HANNAH

Some children who are identified as having special educational needs are successfully included in mainstream classrooms. One such child was Hannah, and the two classroom assistants who worked with other professionals to include Hannah in a mainstream primary school tell Hannah's story in an accessible and practical book called *Working with Hannah*. The account of including Hannah and meeting her specific needs includes details of finding a school, the school's plans and preparations for Hannah, changes and adaptations in the curriculum, Hannah's friendships, arranging and providing therapies during school time, physical care and systems of communication. *Working with Hannah* (Wise and Glass, 2000) is an example of how a young child's specific learning needs can be met and how difficulties and challenges can be overcome.

Nutbrown and Clough (2006: 74), reflecting on inclusive practices with babies and toddlers, argue that to include babies means to find ways to listen to them and become sensitised to their needs and wants:

Such listening is no easy skill to develop for it requires the development of a deep and intimate knowing of each baby – and their ways are different and forms of communication unique. Listening to babies and responding to their interests and impulses requires an attentiveness which is quite different from that needed for work with children who are even only a year older. Let us try to explain what we mean when we say that including babies must begin with listening to them. A childminder took 13 month old Demetrius to watch the trains. She held his hands and patiently supported him as he walked up the steps of the footbridge and bent beside him – her arms around his tummy – as he looked through the railings on the top of the footbridge. In the distance a train was approaching – Demetrius loves the trains and this little outing to watch them go under the bridge was one of his favourite events of any day. As the train came nearer two strangers walked over the footbridge – Demetrius took his eyes off the train and his gaze fixed on the strangers as they approached him, smiled at him and continued past. Demetrius' childminder gently turned his head – reverting his eyes to the train which was about to pass under the bridge. Demetrius struggled slightly in an attempt to continue watching the new people he was so fascinated by, but his childminder had brought him to see the trains and, from her point of view, he was missing the event he usually so enjoyed. What is important here, we suggest, is that listening to babies and toddlers requires constant vigilance and perpetual checking of the adult agenda so that – when children's interest change as subtly as they did for Demetrius – the adult can identify such shifts and further support new interests.

REFERENCES AND INDICATIVE FURTHER READING

Angelides, P. (2000) 'A new technique for dealing with behaviour difficulties in Cyprus: the analysis of critical incidents', *European Journal of Special Needs Education*, 15(1): 55–68.

Barton, L. (1998) *The Politics of Special Educational Needs*. Lewes: Falmer Press.

Berry, T. (2002) 'Does inclusion work? Simon's story', in C. Nutbrown (ed.), *Research Studies in Early Childhood Education*. Stoke-in-Trent. Trentham.

Booth, T. (2000) 'Reflection: Tony Booth', in P. Clough and J. Corbett, *Theories of Inclusive Education*, London: PCP/SAGE.

Booth, T., Ainscow, M., Black-Hawkins, K., Vaughan, M. and Shaw, L. (2002) *Index for Inclusion: developing learning and participation in schools*, 2nd edn. Bristol: Centre for Studies in Inclusive Education.

Brown, B. (1998) *Unlearning Discrimination in the Early Years*. Stoke-on-Trent: Trentham.

Clough, P. (ed.) (1998) *Managing Inclusive Education: From Policy to Experience*. London: PCP/SAGE.

Clough, P. and Corbett, J. (2000) *Theories of Inclusive Education*. London: PCP/SAGE.

Clough, P., Garner, P., Pardeck, J.T. and Yuen, F. (eds) (2004) *Handbook of Emotional and Behavioural Difficulties*. London: Sage.

Corker, M. (2002) 'Profile: Mairian Corker', in P. Clough and J. Corbett, *Theories of Inclusive Education*. London: PCP/SAGE.

Fleer, M. and Williams-Kennedy, D. (2001) *Building Bridges: Literacy Development in Young Indigenous Children*. Canberra: Department of Education, Science and Training.

Gussin Paley, V. (1002) *You Can't Say You Can't Play*. Cambridge, MA: Harvard University Press.

Herbert, E. (1998) 'Included from the start? Managing early years settings for all', in P. Clough (ed.), *Managing Inclusive Education: From Policy to Experience*. London: PCP/SAGE.

Lingard, B. (2000) 'Profile: Bob Lingard', in P. Clough and J. Corbett, *Theories of Inclusive Education*. London: PCP/SAGE.

Lloyd, G., Stead, J., Jordan, E. and Norris, C. (2003) 'Teachers and gypsy travellers', in M. Nind, K. Sheehy and K. Simmons (eds), *Inclusive Education: Learners and Learning Contexts*. London: David Fulton.

Murray, P. and Penman, J. (1996) *Let our Children Be*. Sheffield: Parents with Attitude.

Nutbrown, C. and Clough, P. (2006) *Inclusion in the Early Years: Critical Analyses and Enabling Narratives*. London: Sage.

Visser, J., Cole, T. and Daniels, H. (2003) 'Inclusion for the difficult to include', in M. Nind, K. Sheehy and K.Simmons (eds), *Inclusive Education: Learners and Learning Contexts*. London: David Fulton.

Wise, L. and Glass, C. (2000) *Working with Hannah: A Special Girl in a Mainstream School*. London: RoutledgeFalmer.

In the words of the Introduction the **Index for Inclusion: Developing Play, Learning and Participation in Early Years and Childcare** is 'a detailed set of materials to help settings increase the participation of young children in play and learning' (Booth et al. 2006: 1).

The *Index for Inclusion* was first published in 2000 (Booth et al., 2000) and issued to all schools in the UK. A second edition was published 2002 (Booth et al., 2002) followed, in 2004 by a specially adapted version for use in early years and childcare settings (Booth and Ainscow, 2004) with a second edition published in 2006 (Booth et al., 2006).

> This 2006 revised and updated edition of the Index for early years and childcare now includes a CD Rom to make it more accessible. The Index is a detailed set of materials to help settings increase the participation of children and young people in play and learning. The Index involves a self-review of all aspects of a setting, drawing on additional help as needed. It encourages the involvement in inclusive development of all practitioners, volunteers, management committee/governors, children, young people and their parents/carers. Actions to assist inclusion are prioritized and a development plan is drawn up, implemented and reviewed using the Index materials. These changes are sustained in the setting as the process progresses annually. Within the Index process, practitioners are helped by 46 indicators of inclusion to investigate their culture, policy and practice and to combat all forms of discrimination. These are linked to over 600 questions which allow the setting to be reviewed in detail. (Booth et al., 2006: 1)

The *Index* takes a broad definition of inclusion, stressing participation of *all* children and not just the inclusion of a single group (such as children identified as having Special Educational Needs). The *Index* seeks to support practitioners in developing their own responsiveness (and the responsiveness of the systems in place in the setting) to the diversity of children in those learning communities.

Use of the *Index* is, arguably, a fine example of collective and collaborative action research. Additionally, many issues for research (many of which have themselves arisen from the research of the compilers) arise from using the *Index*. Central research issues are:

- the language and what individuals mean by the term *inclusion*;
- identification of *barriers to play, learning and participation* and identification of ways of reducing discriminatory attitudes and practices and institutional barriers;
- resources to support play, learning and participation within learning communities is a key factor and the need to mobilise resources and maximise use of human resources including children and their parents;
- support for diversity – ways of using support which increases the capacity of the whole setting rather than only identifying support for specific individuals.

Additionally, the *Index* comprises four key 'elements' to support thinking about inclusive development: key concepts, a planning framework, review materials and an inclusive process. The planning framework in the *Index* supports a structured approach to review and development, and suggests ways of working on creating inclusive cultures, producing inclusive policies and evolving inclusive practices. Materials are provided to enable a detailed review of all aspects of a setting and help to identify and implement priorities for change. These materials can make useful survey instruments in themselves as ways of 'taking the pulse' of inclusion within a setting. Using the *Index* is an inclusive process to ensure that the processes of review, planning for change and putting plans into practice are themselves inclusive. Young children, parents, staff and others associated with the provision are included in the process. All of these aspects of the *Index* provide many avenues for research. Key, of course, is the question as to whether and how using the *Index* makes as difference and how that difference is identified in practice.

The following examples are taken from the *Index for Inclusion: Early Years and Childcare* and illustrate how people who have used and are using the *Index* have used the process to understand more of what young children think about the setting they go to.

Learning to listen

We wanted to find out what our children thought about what we were doing for them. We showed some of our five year olds how to use a digital camera and one at a time, asked them to take pictures of things they liked and things they did not like. One girl came back with a picture of the sensory room [a room where children can control experiences of light, sound and touch]. We were very pleased with that room and so I said 'Oh that's something that you really like?' and she said 'no, I don't like it at all'. She said it 'frightened' her. I learnt my lesson, and was careful, from then on, not to jump to conclusions about what the children thought. We also discussed how we could introduce children to the room so that they could choose the level of interaction with it that they felt comfortable with. (Booth and Ainscow, 2004: 29)

Learning how to consult with parents/carers

The practitioners in a playgroup, serving many families on very low incomes, attempted to consult with parents/carers by handing out an adapted questionnaire. Only those parents/carers who helped out regularly replied. The practitioners invited the others, a few at a time, for a cup of tea after a session, explained the purpose of the questionnaire and talked through the main points. With the parents'/carers' agreement they kept a note of opinions expressed. As a result, the practitioners realised that many parents/carers did not feel involved in the playgroup and did not read the information that was given out. They decided to pair practitioners with parents/carers and encourage them to stay behind for a while after sessions to build relationships and offer support. (Booth and Ainscow, 2004: 31)

In a small study which examined the perspectives of five practitioners who used the *Index for Inclusion*, Clough and Nutbrown asked the question: 'Why do we need an Index?' They concluded:

It seems that it is not uncommon to greet yet another development initiative with scepticism; as Helen said: *'another initiative in another glossy folder'*. Yet the five people we spoke to have conveyed something of a personal response to the *Index* which suggests a change *in themselves*. We are left with the impression that there is a great deal of personal interrogation, personal learning, personal change which results as an outcome of engaging with the *Index*. As Pauline says: *we 'think' inclusion now.* Can such changes in thinking, in attitude, in realisation fail to result in changes in practice? If our five participants are in any way typical we have something to learn about the capacity of the *Index* to bring about personal/professional change. As Kay told us: *That whole idea that 'Inclusion' isn't just the latest PC term for SEN – that was really refreshing.*

A key point in the interviews was the development of a shared language for discussion. Sue commented: *We've got a language now to discuss things within the school* and this change in language resulted in Pauline negotiating a change in her title as Special Educational Need Co-ordinator: *I've asked to be called the 'Learning Support Co-ordinator' now. It doesn't really fit, being a SENCO, in an inclusive school!*

Their work with the *Index* in their settings, they told us, made a difference to them as individuals. It was not always easy, as Helen admitted: *It was painful at times. I had to confront and admit some personal prejudices.* But it seems that these early childhood professionals would want to recommend the *Index for Inclusion* to others, in other settings so that they can find out for themselves.

It's not something you can get second hand – you have to be part of the thinking, part of the change. (Clough and Nutbrown, 2003: 92)

REFERENCES AND INDICATIVE FURTHER READING

Booth, T., Ainscow, M., Black-Hawkins, K., Vaughan, M. and Shaw, L. (2000) *Index for Inclusion: Developing Learning and Participation in Schools.* Bristol: Centre for Studies in Inclusive Education.

Booth, T., Ainscow, M., Black-Hawkins, K., Vaughan, M. and Shaw, L. (2002) *Index for Inclusion: Developing Learning and Participation in Schools,* 2nd edn. Bristol: Centre for Studies in Inclusive Education.

Booth, T. and Ainscow, M. (2004) *Index for Inclusion: Developing Learning, Participation and Play in Early Years and Childcare* Bristol: Centre for Studies in Inclusive Education.

Booth, T., Ainscow, M. and Kingston, D. (2006) *Index for Inclusion: Developing Learning, Participation and Play in Early Years and Childcare,* 2nd edn. Bristol: Centre for Studies in Inclusive Education. (The *Index* is available from CSIE, 1 Redland Close, Elm Lane, Redland, Bristol BS6 6UE.)

Clough, P. and Nutbrown, C. (2003) 'The "Index for Inclusion": perspectives of early years practitioners'; in M. Nind, K. Sheehy and K. Simmons (eds), *Inclusive Education: Learners and Learning Contexts.* London: David Fulton.

A 'Key Person' is someone identified in group day care who has specific responsibility for a number of named children. She or he liaises with parents and attends to all aspects of the young child's needs and development while in the setting. The Key Person develops a close relationship, with the children to whom she or he is 'key' and thus detailed knowledge of their needs.

The constant debate about attachments has for years led many staff in nurseries to shy away from close attachments with children, fearing that the parent will be unable to cope with the idea that another person outside the family has a close relationship with their baby. Many parents who choose childcare in a nursery, as opposed to childminders or nannies, do so because they fear the child will form a close attachment to an individual carer, thus ostracising the parent and exacerbating their feelings of guilt about returning to work and leaving a young child in 'paid for' care for a major part of their waking day.

The idea of a 'Key Person' is that an individual member of the staff team is designated to work with and care for specific children and to liaise with their parents, forming – in some cases – a complex triangle of relationships and creating intimate interactions between child and practitioner and (often) practitioner and parent. Research suggests that in good quality settings, children benefit from early education and care, thus contesting earlier concerns about emotional attachment (DfEE, 1998; Moss and Melhuish, 1991). It is considered, in many settings, to be good practice to identify a 'Key Person' for each baby and young child who can provide continuity of care and lessen anxiety around separation from his or her parent (Goldschmied and Jackson, 2003; Nutbrown and Page, 2008; Penn, 1999).

It could be argued, then, that there are too many reasons not to implement a Key Person approach in a nursery, if the designation of a person who will have major responsibility for a child carries with it the danger of enhanced anxiety for the parents and, by default, the practitioner (Goldschmied and Jackson, 2003).

However, Elfer et al. (2003) argue to the contrary. They claim that the benefits to the child are overwhelming. Moreover, they offer that the complex relationship difficulties surrounding the implementation of a Key Person approach are 'Challenges to be overcome, rather than reasons *not* to develop the Key Person approach' (Elfer et al., 2003: 12).

> We introduce and argue the case for a Key Person approach and describe the benefits for everyone involved. We explain how any nursery can develop such an approach, whereby one or two adults in the nursery, while never taking over from parents, connect with what parents would ordinarily do: being special for the children, helping them manage throughout the day, thinking about them, getting to know them well, and sometimes worrying about them too – all of which help a child to make a strong link between home and nursery. We have called the person who bears that role the child's *Key Person*. The organisational set-up within the setting that makes it all happen is the *Key Person approach*. (Elfer et al., 2003: vi)

Further examples are provided by practitioners working in group care settings where a Key Person approach operates. The same practitioner works with the same baby each day, feeding, changing nappies and interacting with the baby in a close, respectful and dignified manner. By observing children closely, the adult can ensure that the views of the child are respected and upheld, irrespective of the age of the child.

> In many families, nurseries and neighbourhoods we are not used to giving weight to the views of children of any age, especially not to babies under a year old. If we are to be strong advocates for children then we need to observe and interpret the preferences and ideas of children especially those who don't yet communicate with language (Goldschmied and Selleck, 1996: 3–4)

Gillespie Edwards (2002) continues this theme acknowledging the fears and anxiety that some practitioners may experience. Furthermore she suggests that the Key Person approach requires planning and the frequent revisiting of nursery policies to support both the child/ren and the practitioner particularly with regard to child protection. She explores both the practicalities and the complexities of the role of the key person. But nevertheless she states emphatically that babies and children require: 'being physically held and caressed ... An attachment relationship is one of intimacy, involving all the senses' (Gillespie Edwards,

2002: 22.) She points out that the Key Person's role is exhausting and demanding. It clearly involves more than just caring for the physical needs of the child. 'Physical care for the youngest children is personalised, being based on not only the child's physical needs, but also on sensitive observation of the child's emotional state and knowledge of her preferred routines. (Gillespie Edwards, 2002: 47)

Messages about the importance of close emotional attachments were also clearly echoed in the 'Development matters' section of the component 'Emotional well-being' within the 'Healthy Child' aspect of *Birth to Three Matters: A Framework of Support for Our Youngest Children* (DfES, 2003). 'Young babies are social beings. They crave close attachments with a special person within their setting' (DfES, 2003).

Despite some agreement about the Key Person being 'a good thing' for the very youngest children, there is very little work on the impact of the development of close attachments on the professional so involved. As Goldschmied and Selleck note: 'Powerful feelings that may include jealousy and rivalry will need to be acknowledged and supported in a careful management programme of support and supervision for the key people' (1996: 47).

The role of the practitioner is crucial in caring for and educating young children. Adults who are 'in tune' with children are better able to support their learning, and it could be argued that the provision of a Key Person should be afforded to children as a matter of right. Reflecting on the implications of the UN Convention on the Rights of the Child for provision for young children, Page (2005: 100) argues that 'parents and practitioners can empower young children and respect their rights by creating a respectful environment and by giving them a choice'. Further, Page argues that the Key Person approach is essential if children are to feel secure and loved in their early years settings (Nutbrown and Page, 2008).

Available examples of young children and their key workers are useful in understanding the play dynamic which develops and how the relationship an intimacy they share can enhance children's learning.

Jane was working with three-year-old Allen and four-month-old Naomi. Allen wanted Naomi to hold a set of plastic keys. Jane gently reminded Allen that Naomi was allowed to choose what she played with (she seemed to prefer to suck her soft bunny at the time). Jane said to Allen, 'She can choose, she doesn't have to play with the one you like, you like to choose, she likes to choose as well'. Jane knew Allen so well that she was confident that this explanation would help him to understand that babies have opportunities for choice as well as children who were older. Allen recognised this assertion and went away. He returned with a small selection of toys which he put at the side of baby Naomi: 'There – now she can choose.'

Nadia was seven months old. She was sitting in her high chair eating a plate of pasta and peas. Using her left hand she carefully picked up each piece of pasta with her fingers and ate them until only the peas were left on the plate. Then she ate the peas, one at a time, picking up each one with her fingers, looking at it closely before putting it in her mouth. Lunch lasted much longer for Nadia than it did for some of the other children in the group, but her key worker knew that Nadia needed to take her time and focus carefully and quietly on her food. The adult knew, because she had spent so many mealtimes with Nadia, that this was a part of the day not to be hurried, but to be quietly and calmly enjoyed!

REFERENCES AND INDICATIVE FURTHER READING

DfEE (1998) *Meeting the Childcare Challenge: A Framework and Consultation Document*. London: DfEE.

DfES (2003) *Birth to Three Matters: A Framework of Support for Our Youngest Children*. London: DfES/Sure Start.

Elfer, P. Goldschmied, E. and Selleck, D. (2003) *Key Persons in the Nursery: Building Relationships for Quality Provision*. London: David Fulton.

Gillespie Edwards, A. (2002) *Relationships and Learning: Caring for Children from Birth to Three*. London: National Children's Bureau.

Goldschmied, E. and Jackson, S. (2003) *People Under Three: Young Children in Day Care*, 2nd edn. London: Routledge.

Goldschmied, E. and Selleck, D. (1996) *Communication Between Babies in Their First Year*. London: National Children's Bureau.

Moss, P. and Melhuish, E. (1991) *Current Issues in Day Care for Young Children*. London: HMSO.

Nutbrown, C. and Page, J. (2008) *Working with Babies and Children: From Birth to Three*. London: Sage.

Page, J. (2005) 'Working with children under three: the perspectives of three UK academics', in K. Hirst and C. Nutbrown (eds), *Perspectives on Early Childhood Education: Essays in Contemporary Research*. Stoke-on-Trent: Trentham.

Penn, H. (1999) *How Should We Care for Babies and Toddlers? An Analysis of Practice in Out-of-home Settings for Children Under Three*. Occasional Paper 10.6.1999 iv. Childcare Resource and Research Unit, University of Toronto, Canada.

> Media and popular culture, in early childhood education and care, refers to the use of media (television, video, DVD and other information and communication technologies [ICTs], including new digital technologies) – and related artefacts, in children's home lives and in education and care settings.

The twenty-first century is a digital age, and much of the world relies heavily on technology in a way which previous generations have never experienced. With the growth of digital technology the early experiences of many children have changed. Television is common in most households, where it is now unusual to own only one television set. Many children have their own television and video/DVD-playing equipment in their bedrooms, and there are dedicated television channels for children. New digital technologies on mobile phones and the Internet have brought about the growth of media-based popular culture as an integral and somewhat unexamined part, of children's lives.

The term 'popular culture' in the context of recent early childhood research is generally taken to mean texts and artefacts which are mass produced and known to, used and owned by, many young children. Popular television programmes, for example, are often linked by the producers to dolls, figures, books or comics, lunch boxes, T-shirts, bed covers, wallpaper, and so on (Kenway and Bullen, 2001). As Marsh puts it:

Children's popular culture is often considered to be subject to the 'McDonaldisation' effect (Ritzer, 1998) in that it is assumed that US-based themes dominate the global market. However, this is often not the case, as the worldwide popularity of the *Teletubbies* (of UK origin) and *Pokemon* (of Japanese origin) attest. In short, this is a complex area in which assumptions made are often erroneous and the dynamic interplay between globalising and localising effects overlooked. In addition, it is important to note that culture is also produced, not simply consumed. Although children's culture is often shaped by adults and taken up by children (or not, as the case may be) in various ways, children also create their own, child-centred cultural practices. Ultimately, definitions of children's popular culture depend on a sensitive reading of socio-cultural practices in specific contexts. (Marsh, 2005a: 3)

A number of researchers have demonstrated the force of popular culture in the development of children's literacy. Dyson, for example, shows how television 'superheroes' can fuel children's writing (Dyson, 1997, 2002). The growth of popular culture is undoubtedly linked with the development and relatively easy acquisition of recently introduced digital technologies and so the term 'new media' is used by some to refer to the increasing range of activities and tools which employ and exploit popular culture through the use of digital and other technology. Within this, computer technology has had an increasing impact on the development of children's electronic and computer-based toys, and on their experiences of moving images and interactive technologies in their own home and in group education and care settings. DVDs, video cameras and voice-activated technology – to name but a few – are familiar to, and even taken for granted, by many young children.

Jenkinson (2001) argues that excessive television watching is a serious threat to children's healthy development, with television having a detrimental effect on children's physical and mental health, citing a range of studies which raise concerns about children's: obesity, inactivity, violent/aggressive behaviour, desensitisation (to real-life events) and sexual attitude/behaviour.

Concerns in the US led to the publication of *Fool's Gold* (Cordes and Miller, 2000) a report which warned of the dangers of young children using new media technology including:

- hazards to children's physical health (skeletal development, vision problems, obesity, toxic emissions and electromagnetic radiation);
- risks to emotional and social development (children leading isolated television and computer-oriented lives, limited self-motivation, detachment from community, the commercialisation of childhood);
- risks to creativity and intellectual development (limited imagination, loss of wonder, limited language and literacy development, poor concentration, limited capacity for hard work, plagiarism of others' ideas, distraction from meaning);
- risks to moral development.

Cordes and Miller (2000) promote the development of close loving relationships, play, outdoor activity, handcrafts, conversation, poetry and storytelling with loving adults as essential alternatives to media and popular culture for young children in their early years of childhood.

In a study for the BBC's *Child of Our Time* series, Marsh (2005b) argues that children live a balanced social and cultural life which includes watching television, videos and DVD, playing video games and using computers, but also includes playing with toys, playing outdoors and listening to stories read to them. Though it is difficult for parents and carers to 'steer a path through this rather confusing mixture of media hype and moral panic', Marsh asks 'Haven't things always been this way? The adult world has often looked on the new practices of childhood with some anxiety, each generation thinking that the next one will be corrupted by new pastimes'. An Australian study of 20 children (ten boys and ten girls) aged 14–24 months, watching an episode of the television programme *Teletubbies* highlighted interactive and responsive skills (Roberts and Howard, 2005). These young children's attentive responses were very strong and they made meaningful connections between the programme and their own lives. The authors write:

> We have shown our young participants using a television text both for pleasure and for making sense of their worlds and in this they are no different from older children. Indeed we would suggest that programmes like *Teletubbies* enable very young viewers to exercise and develop those skills and dispositions that make older brothers and sisters savvy operators in a pervasive media environment. (Roberts and Howard, 2005: 106)

The following examples shows how early years practitioners have used children's interest in popular television culture to extend the curriculum in ways which appeared meaningful to the children and allowed them to bring their cultural capital to the classroom.

The underwater classroom

Many of the children in the class had seen the Disney film *Finding Nemo* (Disney/Pixar, 2003). They were attracted to the idea of an underwater school but appalled by the idea of being taken from the ocean and confined to a small tank. The spontaneous playtime game of a group of children involved playing underwater schools. They 'swam' around the outdoor playground singing nursery rhymes and searching for 'Nemo'. The teacher encouraged the children to extend their ideas into the classroom, asking them to design underwater classrooms and to imagine what it would be like if their own school was under the sea. How would they get there? What would they wear? What kinds of lessons would they have? The outcomes were some imaginative stories and classroom designs – and 'swim time' instead of 'playtime'. Having researched the different types of fish featured in the film, they cast various members of staff as different types of sea creatures. The head teacher was a manta ray and their own teacher a very pink lobster (they did not ask why!).

Maisie's Teletubbies

In another classroom a practitioner asked the children to each make a list of all the things they had at home which were connected with a television character. Many lists were long, and the children needed some help to record some of the complex terms they wanted to use. What emerged was that most of the children were surrounded with books and objects which were part of their popular and media culture. Figure 4 shows Maisie's list which begins with the names of the four soft toy dolls who are the *Teletubbies*.

Maisie's Teletubby things:

Tinky Winky
Dipsy
La La
Po
Lunch box with Teletubbies on
Teletubby jamas
Two videos
Teletubby book - the big one
Crayoning book
Stickers
Pillow case (mummy couldn't find the quilt cover
    but she'll get it for me)
Little tiny Teletubby toys and their kitchen
Jigsaw with Tinky Winky and rabbits
Rabbit (a real one called La La)
Pencils
Felt tips
Wellies with Tellytubby stickers on
Teletubby T-shirt - it's pink!
Teletubby baseball hat for the summer
... and I'm getting a Teletubby bike for my
birthday (I think I am!)

Figure 4   *Maisie's Teletubby list*

REFERENCES AND INDICATIVE FURTHER READING

Cordes, C. and Millar, E. (2000) *Fool's Gold: A Critical look at Computers in Childhood*. College Park, MD: Alliance for Childhood.

Disney/Pixar (2003) *Finding Nemo (DVD)*.

Dyson. A.H. (1997) *Writing Superheroes: Contemporary Childhood, Popular Culture and Classroom Literacy*. New York: Teachers College Press.

Dyson, A.H. (2002) *Brothers and Sisters Learn to Write: Popular Literacies in Childhood and School Cultures*. New York: Teachers College Press.

Jenkinson, S. (2001) *The Genius of Play: Celebrating the Spirit of Childhood*. Stroud: Hawthorn Press.

Kenway, M. and Bullen, E. (2001) *Consuming Children: Education – Entertainment – Advertising*. Buckingham: Open University Press.

Marsh, J. (ed.) (2005a) *Popular Culture, New Media and Digital Literacy in Early Childhood*. London: RoutledgeFalmer.

Marsh, J. (2005b) 'Digikids: young children, popular culture and media', in N. Yelland (ed.), *Critical Issues in Early Childhood Education*. Buckingham: Open University Press.

Marsh, J. and Thompson, P. (2001) 'Parental involvement in literacy development using media texts', *Journal of Research in Reading*, 24(3): 266–78.

Ritzer, G. (1998) *The McDonaldisation Thesis: Explorations and Extensions*. London: Sage.

Roberts, S. and Howard, S. (2005) 'Watching Teletubbies: television and its very young audience', in J. Marsh (ed.), *Popular Culture, New Media and Digital Literacy in Early Childhood*. London: RoutledgeFalmer.

media and popular culture

> *The Montessori Method describes the practices and pedagogy of early education developed by Maria Montessori. These practices are now adopted – to varying degrees – in many early years settings which bear her name.*

Maria Montessori (1870–1952) was an Italian medical doctor who worked with children with learning difficulties in socially deprived areas of Rome. In 1907 she began work with 50 children living in the slum areas of Rome who, within two years, were considered to be achieving educationally alongside other children of their age. Her success brought her worldwide acclaim.

From her early work, Montessori developed a set of principles, based on her observation of these children, which she argued were applicable to the learning of all children. The Montessori Method is based on a philosophy which encompasses a range of issues, namely: multi-age grouping of children according to periods of development; human tendencies; the process of children's learning; the prepared environment; observation; work centres; teaching method; class size; basic lessons; areas of study; daily schedule; assessment; learning styles, and character education.

Within these many elements the notion of 'human tendencies' is perhaps key. Montessori developed her methods by building on her observations that learning is brought about by human tendencies to do – to act, to explore, to create. She observed that learning happened through repetition, concentration, imagination, and that learners needed to be independent in their actions while making their own decisions about what 'work' they should do and learning how to control their own actions.

Reflecting on her approach Montessori wrote:

> Like others I had believed that it was necessary to encourage a child by means of some exterior reward that would flatter his baser sentiments, such as gluttony, vanity, or self-love, in order to foster in him a spirit of work and peace. And I was astonished when I learned that a child who is

permitted to educate himself really gives up these lower instincts. I then urged the teachers to cease handing out the ordinary prizes and punishments, which were no longer suited to our children, and to confine themselves to directing them gently in their work.

The Montessori Method suggests that children aged three to six years work for those years with the same teacher, the aim being to work and learn in an environment which has been created and prepared by the teacher to encourage socialisation and learning which involves solving problems, children teaching other children and interaction. In some countries this aim is not fulfilled because children leave their Montessori setting to attend mainstream school around the age of five (sometimes earlier). There are a small number of Montessori reception classes which continue to teach according to Montessorian principles. An underpinning premise of the Montessori Method was that children should direct their own learning and that teachers should 'follow the child'.

Montessori was, undoubtedly, a pioneer in the field of childcare and education and, though famous for her influence on early childhood education, her work included ways of working with children of all ages. Montessorian approaches are used, internationally, in education settings and in home-based provision for children.

The Montessorian view of the Process of Learning is seen as having three stages:

Stage 1 Introduction of a concept by means of a lesson or other form.
Stage 2 Processing the information gained in Stage 1 and coming to an understanding of the concept through the processes of doing, experimenting, making. This stage can take some time and involve much discovery, repetition and interaction.
Stage 3 'Knowing' – being about to use the concept learned to pass it on, to teach another child, to show someone or to discuss it with clear competence.

Basic lessons and 'work' are central elements of Montessori teaching. Many prepared materials are designed to teach children processes of work: cleaning, cooking and so on. To this end, substantial periods of time are made over to children selecting from the prepared materials, carrying out the task they have chosen and moving from area to area, working on the materials they choose without the constraints of other timetabled events.

Much of the teaching is carried out on an individual basis, the teacher intervening, based on her or his observations and tuning into individual children's learning styles. Teachers foster concentration and neither they, nor other children are encouraged to interrupt a child who is busy working on the materials she or he has selected.

Well known for her distinctive work on early childhood curriculum and pedagogy, Maria Montessori was also well respected in the world of science, being invited to the US in 1915 by Alexander Graham Bell and Thomas Edison to address an audience at the Carnegie Hall. She was politically active and her expression of anti-fascist views forced her into exile during the Second World War. She was twice nominated for the Nobel Peace Prize and, until the adoption by Italy of the euro, her face appeared on the 1000 lire note in recognition and honour of her achievements.

The Montessori Method gives rise to a number of research questions, and among them is the question as to how children who attend Montessori nurseries fare when they transfer to a mainstream, non-Montessorian, school environment. Barber (2005) examined the attitudes and responses of Montessori teachers and mainstream reception classes towards the transition of children from a Montessori setting to mainstream classes at the age of five. She found that the children from Montessori classes coped well, but also identified the need for a greater exchange of information so that reception class teachers understood the experiences that Montessori-educated children had, and could therefore prepare for their entry into school.

Internationally, issues for research include cultural compatibility and the ways in which the Montessori approach can be adapted to ensure that the environment and learning tasks are culturally appropriate. Work has also been developed in some settings to include children with learning difficulties – more understanding of this approach to Inclusion is needed.

Three-year-old Samir chooses a tray from the shelf of his Montessori kindergarten. He takes it to a low table and sits down. On the small tray are two china bowls, one containing rice, and a spoon. Samir has chosen this tray before and he knows what to do. He begins, slowly and carefully, scooping the rice with a spoon and transferring it from one bowl to another. He works silently, a teacher nearby is working with another child, she looks up occasionally, aware of what he is doing. She does not interfere or interrupt. Samir completes the task, returns the tray to the shelf and walks around the room while deciding what he wishes to work on next.

Amy is four and a half years old. She is working with a set of cylinders with which she is very familiar. She is sitting on a small mat, on the floor. She seems to know that the wooden cylinders, each a different size, will each only fit into one of the spaces in the accompanying tray. She works quickly and deftly. She glances up and sees another child, seemingly struggling, with a similar piece of equipment. Silently she approaches the child, and moves one cylinder into the correct hole. The younger child looks at her, smiles (as he has understood what was going wrong) and continues the task he has chosen, eventually with success. Amy returns to her cylinders, completes the task and returns the cylinders to their shelf. She folds up her mat and places it with the other mats in a nearby box.

REFERENCES AND INDICATIVE FURTHER READING

Barber, H. (2005) 'Joining the "mainstream": transferring from a Montessori nursery school to a state reception class', in K. Hirst and C. Nutbrown (eds), *Perspectives on Early Childhood Education: Contemporary Research*. Stoke-in-Trent: Trentham.

Lillard, P.P. (1973) *Montessori: A Modern Approach*. New York: Schocken Books.

Montessori, M. (1914) *Dr Montessori's Own Handbook*. New York: Schocken Books.

Montessori, M. (1962) *Education for a New World*. Wheaton, IL: Theosophical Press.

Montessori, M. (1963) *The Secret of Childhood*. Calcutta: Orient Longmans.

Montessori, M. (1964) *The Absorbent Mind*. Wheaton, IL: Theosophical Press.

Montessori, M. (1964) *The Montessori Method*. New York: Schocken Books.

montessori method

> *The study of neuro-systems in the brains of young babies, which has led to suggested implications for practice in early childhood education and care.*

According to recent scientific research, babies and young children are born with the capacity to understand a lot more than was previously thought to be the case. 'We've learned more in the last thirty years about what babies and young children know than we did in the preceding 2,500 years' (Gopnik et al., 1999: 22). It was not long ago that we were told that newborn babies do not feel pain, or that young children find it impossible to see the world from anything but their own perspective (David, 1999: 87), but new science-based studies, which have used video-observational work of babies have challenged this view. 'By using videotape we can objectively measure what babies do and look at it slowly, over and over' (Gopnik et al., 1999: 21).

Recent studies have challenged the long-held view of babies' 'ignorance' suggesting that babies, indeed, have an innate capacity from the moment they are born. More is understood now about questions such as whether babies get 'bored', whether they can recognise faces and whether they can differentiate between objects. Using video recordings of newborn babies in controlled situations, independent observers have noted and analysed such things as eye movements to see which pictures babies appear to prefer. Experiments such as these suggest that babies can recognise different faces within a few days of birth. The process of 'habituation' (Brierley, 1994: 81; Gopnik et al., 1999: 27) confirms the importance of providing babies with novelty and stimulation in their environments. As Brierley (1994: 82) noted: 'The brain thrives on variety and stimulation. Monotony of surroundings, toys that only do one thing are soon disregarded by the brain'. A number of similar experiments have been carried out to establish the levels of understanding that babies and young children have throughout the first three years of their lives.

Studies regarding the relationship between a newborn child and his or her mother have been used to identify the complex capacity of babies

(Anon., 2002: 3). Bruner's 1960 theory of 'cognitive growth' suggested that environmental and experiential factors were influences on a child's development (Smith, 2002b). Trevarthen's (1977), focus on the communication of five babies during their first six months of life concluded that a pattern of development in social behaviour was forming in all five infants.

Gopnik et al. (1999) suggest that despite the extensive experiments that have taken place in a bid to prove one theory over another, it is at times difficult to grasp the amazing phenomenon of how young children think. They summarise this notion in terms of three elements:

- *Foundation* where babies are able to translate information and interpret their experiences in particular ways predicting new events;
- *Learning* when babies use their experiences to modify and reshape their initial representation thus achieving more complex and abstract representations;
- *Other people* who care for the children actively yet, unconsciously promote, encourage and influence children's representations.

However, there are limitations to what neuroscience can offer early childhood education and care. Hannon (2003) argues that while the results of the studies of neuroscience are interesting: 'They have limited implications for early childhood intervention and education in the sense of changing what is currently already done on the basis of non-neuroscience research or custom' (Hannon, 2003: 8).

Wilson (2002) suggests that brain science has little to offer parents, and the factors impacting on childhood outcomes are complex and cannot be reduced solely to biomedical explanations. Wilson argues that child health and welfare problems, for example, would more effectively involve a multidimensional approach and include the elimination of poverty and the scrutiny of public policy in relation to young children and families.

If children are born with innate tendencies, it is important that adults harness and support those skills in order for children to continue their educational path in a learning environment. Learning environments and inter-personal relationships become crucial. Further studies of the role of the Key Person and the environments provided for babies are needed in order to maximise practices and inform the development of future policies in order that provision for young children and information provided to parents is of the kind which will make the most of children's potential and best meet their needs.

By the age of about 12 months babies will be influenced by the actions of an adult when they are introduced to a new experience. If a child is offered a new toy, s/he may look for reassurance from a familiar adult before attempting to play with it. If the adult looks unsure, the baby may be put off from exploring any further (Gopnik et al., 1999). This identifies the importance of the role of a familiar adult and emphasises the crucial role of the adult in scaffolding the child's learning. Future research needs to find ways of supporting adults in developing their unique roles in the education and care of babies.

Scottish policy on provision and work with children under three demonstrates how practices can be underpinned by an understanding of neuroscience. A summary of findings from brain studies with implications for practice includes the following:

Within the first three years of life, most babies quickly learn to interact with others around them, to walk, to talk and to solve problems at a truly amazing rate. Research into brain development in recent years has established that:

- learning takes place within the womb before a baby is even born
- babies are born with a powerful motivation and ability to learn
- young children's brains develop very rapidly and the responses that babies and young children receive from the others around them actively promote this rapid development
- from birth, babies' brains are ready to begin making connections and many important connections are made in the first three years of life by being active and involved, by learning through exploration, discovery and interactions with others, development takes place.

Research has important implications for the ways in which adults support, care and provide for very young children. It reminds us that it is important not to underestimate the competence of even the youngest child. ... Babies and young children learn positively and begin to make sense of the world through warm and accepting relationships, through enjoyable play and from being involved in everyday routines. Although young children have similar basic needs, all babies and children are unique individuals. Understanding what is unique about each child you care for allows you to meet children's needs in the special and individual way that supports the individual's development and learning. For example, all babies and children need food, warmth, affection and stimulation. However, there will be many variations in the way that individual babies like to be fed and differences in what they like to eat; there will be differences in the way that babies allow themselves to be comforted and soothed and differences in the ways that babies ask for and accept affection.

There will be differences in the ways and the pace at which they learn. This is because they are all individuals and one approach for all will not be appropriate or effective.

Young children need intimate and flexible environments, with *other people*, who will give them time and attention, who will show a genuine interest and delight in them … (Learning and Teaching Scotland, 2005: 23)

REFERENCES AND INDICATIVE FURTHER READING

Anon. (2002) *Intersubjectivity*. Available at: www.geocities.com/Athens/Acopo..inter-subjectivity.htm

Bowlby, J. (1965) *Child Care and the Growth of Love*, 2nd edn. Harmondsworth Penguin Books.

Bowlby, J. (1984) *Attachment and loss: Volume 1 Attachment*, 2nd edn. London: Penguin Books.

Brierley, J. (1994) *Give me a child until he is seven: Brain Studies & Early Childhood Education*, 2nd edn. London: Falmer Press.

David, T. (1999) 'Valuing young children', in L. Abbott and H. Moylett (eds), *Early Education Transformed*. London: Falmer Press.

Gardner, H. (1983) *Frames of Mind: The Theory of Multiple Intelligences*. New York: Basic Books.

Gopnik, A. Meltzoff, A. and Kuhl, P. (1999) *How Babies Think*. London: Weindenfeld & Nicholson.

Hannon, P. (2003) 'Developmental neuroscience: implications for early childhood intervention and education', *Current Paediatrics*. 13: 23–31.

Hoy, G. (1998) *Multiple Intelligences and Emotional Literacy*. Available at: www.feel. org/articles/multiple_intelligences.html

Learning and Teaching Scotland (2005) *Birth to Three: Supporting our Youngest Children*. Edinburgh: Learning and Teaching Scotland.

Rutter, M. (1972) *Maternal Deprivation Reassessed*. Harmondsworth: Penguin Books.

Smith, M.K. (2002a) *Howard Gardner and Multiple Intelligences: The Encyclopaedia of Informal Education*. Available at: www.infed.org/thinkers/gardner.htm (accessed July 2005).

Smith, M.K. (2002b) *Jerome S. Bruner and the Process of Education: The Encyclopaedia of Informal Education*. www.infed.org/thinkers/bruner.htm (accessed July 2005).

Tobias, S. (2000) 'The feelings of vocabulary', *The Children's Emotional Literacy Project*. Available at: www.kidseq.com/articles.html (last updated 26 September 2000).

Trevarthen, C. (1977) 'Descriptive analyses of infant communicative behaviour', in H.R. Schaffer (ed.), *Studies in Mother–Infant Interaction*. London: Academic Press.

Trevarthen, C. (1978) 'Secondary intersubjectivity: confidence, confiding and acts of meaning in the first year', in A. Lock (ed.), *Action, Gesture and Symbol. The Emergence of Language.* London: Academic Press.

Trevarthen, C. (1992) 'An infant's motives for speaking and thinking in the culture', in A.H. Wold (ed.), *The Dialogical Alternative.* Oxford: Oxford University Press. pp. 99–137.

Wilson, H. (2002) 'Brain science, early intervention and "at risk" families: implications for parents, professionals and social policy', *Social Policy and Society,* 1(3): 191–202.

parental involvement

Parental involvement in young children's learning now refers to the myriad of programmes, systems and practices in place in early years settings and schools to value parents' roles in their own children's learning and development and to encourage such involvement in the setting and at home.

Research and practice in the past two decades have shed light on parents' roles in their own children's learning and prompted the development of practices and programmes to involve parents more systematically in their own children's education. Though it is difficult to identify precise beginnings, parental involvement in their children's learning has, for some time, been part of working with young children. It is known, for example, that Margaret McMillan included 'lectures' for parents in her development of nursery schools. During the 1960s, programmes to involve parents began to be developed – largely as a way of addressing poor home experiences. However, as it is currently understood, parental involvement could perhaps be traced back to the Rumbold Report, *Starting with Quality* (DES, 1990), which promoted the idea that parents were their children's first and most important educators. Current government policy makes it clear that involvement with parents is an expected part of early childhood education and care in all settings:

> Parents are children's first and most enduring educators. When parents and practitioners work together in early years settings, the results have a positive impact on the child's development and learning. Therefore, each setting should seek to develop an effective partnership with parents. (QCA, 2000)

There are many examples of parental involvement in children's learning, and, as recent examples have shown (Draper and Duffy, 2001; Nutbrown et al., 2005, Whalley, 1997) the model of parental involvement is largely participative – a far cry from the compensatory ethos which dominated early programmes of the 1960s. and 1970s.

Hurst and Joseph (2003) viewed the coming together of parents and practitioners as 'sharing education'. They argued for understanding of the complex cultural differences and shifts which children, parents and practitioners experienced when they entered each other's worlds and opportunities for each to 'share' the others. However,

> The sharing of intentions and perspectives between parents and practitioners is not easy in a busy classroom. There has to be a rationale for it, and it needs links with a curriculum model which sets a value on children's experiences at home with family and friends. It requires just as much commitment as sharing intentions with children does. Contacts with the home should be seen as a part of the curriculum, and a part of the practitioner's responsibility to provide for children's learning in ways that suit them. The first step is to consider what kind of contact with parents is most valuable, and to find out what kind of contact with the setting is needed by the parents. (Hurst and Joseph, 2003: 89)

Specific initiatives to involve parents in the early years have often focused on young children's learning or aspects of curriculum and helping parents learn more about their children's ways of learning. The Froebel Early Learning Project, (Athey, 2007) identified ways of helping parents to understand their children's learning interests so that they could better support them. This theme is further developed by Nutbrown (2011), who argued that the more parents know about how children's learning developed, the better position they were in to understand what their children were doing and how they might further enhance learning opportunities for them. More recently the PEEP project in oxfordshire, has developed ways of involving parents with babies and young children in several aspects of their learning and development (Roberts 2001).

A recent study of work with parents to promote early literacy development has used the ORIM conceptual framework to focus on four main ways in which parents can help their children's literacy development (Figure 5), by providing *Opportunities, Recognition, Interaction* and a *Model* for their children.

OPPORTUNITIES

In the early years, parents can provide vital learning opportunities for their children's literacy development by:

- resourcing children's drawing and writing activities;
- encouraging their socio-dramatic play;
- exposing them to, and helping them interpret, environmental print;
- exposing them to nursery rhymes and other word-play rhymes or songs which aid speech segmentation and phonological awareness;
- ensuring that story books and other written materials are available with time and space to use them;
- enabling children to participate in visits, trips or holidays which provide further opportunities to talk, read and write.

STRANDS OF EARLY LITARACY DEVELOPMENT

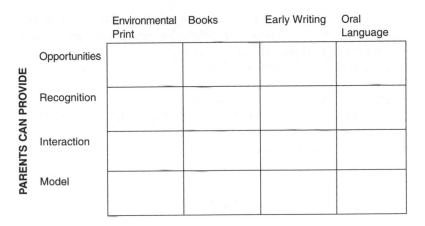

	Environmental Print	Books	Early Writing	Oral Language
Opportunities				
Recognition				
Interaction				
Model				

(PARENTS CAN PROVIDE)

Figure 5   *The ORIM framework*

RECOGNITION

It is important that parents are aware of, and can identify, early milestones in development as well as the achievement of clear stages in literacy learning. Parents can provide unique encouragement for children if they show recognition; their value, appreciation and understanding, of children's early literacy achievements by, for example:

- praising children when they 'read' a book;
- putting their writing or drawing on show (on the 'fridge, kitchen wall, etc.);
- telling others (granny, auntie, etc.) what the child has done or achieved.

INTERACTION

Children need their parents to spend time with them, supporting, explaining, endorsing and challenging them to move on from what they know about literacy to do more. An important part of such interaction is the sharing of real-life literacy tasks where children can make a meaningful contribution, for example:

- adding their name or mark to a birthday card;
- helping to write a shopping list;
- helping to find particular items in the shops;
- turning the pages of a book while a parent reads.

Through such interactions parents will enable their children to progress from what they can do now with help to becoming more independent in the future (Vygotsky, 1978).

Other forms of interaction include:

- showing children *how* to do something;
- deliberately *teaching* a child something – for example how to write his or her name;
- playing word/letter/sound games;
- participating in socio-dramatic play.

MODELS

Parents can act as powerful models of users of literacy if and when children see them using literacy themselves in everyday life. For example:

- reading a newspaper or magazine;
- doing the crossword;
- writing notes or shopping lists;
- following a cooking recipe;
- following instructions for assembling furniture or how to work a piece of equipment;
- writing cheques;
- filling in forms;
- signing their name.

The four concepts and the specific actions attached to them form the key roles parents can play in enhancing their children's literacy development.

Others have developed the ORIM framework to incorporate other aspects of development (Delaney, 1997; Fagan, 2000; Preece, 1999; Rigo-Toth and Ure, 2000; Roberts, 2001; Turnbull, 1998).

Key issues for research continue to be how to involve parents in ways which are inclusive, participative, respectful and meaningful. Some settings have developed an international reputation for their work in involving parents in their children's learning, for example the Pen Green Centre (Arnold, 2001; Whalley and the Pen Green Centre Team, 1997) the Coram Children's Centre in London (Draper and Duffy, 2001) and the Sheffield Children's Centre. Most recently, Sure Start projects have involved parents in a range of programmes to support them in promoting babies and young children's health, physical, social, emotional and cognitive development. Many settings develop their own specific projects to help parents learn more about their children's learning, such as that reported by Parker (2002) who explains how sharing work with parents on children's drawing and mark-making led to enhanced understanding and enthusiasm from parents. Parker records the views of some parents who remarked:

I have been able to enter her imagination and see the world through her eyes.

Now I'm fascinated by the way she develops a drawing, rather than just looking at the end result.

I have learnt that Brandon is more capable of mark making than I first thought. (Parker, 2002: 92)

Parker notes:

The parents learned from observing their children and developed an appreciation of their children's high levels of involvement, discussing their children's achievements at home with confidence, clarity and joy ... The children have been the primary beneficiaries of this collaboration between parents and practitioners. We all had valuable knowledge and understanding to share. This was a group which enjoyed mutual respect, shared understandings, political awareness and a commitment to extending learning opportunities for young children. (Parker, 2002: 92–3)

In some cases initiatives have been targeted specifically at minority groups, including families for whom English is not the language of the home. Karran (2003) describes work with parents who are learning English as an additional language and the importance of bilingual support for such parents who want to understand more of education systems and how to help their young children. Siraj-Blatchford (1994) has argued that in some cultures 'education' and 'home' are distinct and separate and time may need to be given to explaining how home–school partnerships can support young children's learning and development. Baz et al. (1997) have discussed the importance of bilingual early childhood educators working bilingually with parents and young children using books, early writing, rhymes and poems in families' homes and in group settings.

REFERENCES AND INDICATIVE FURTHER READING

Arnold, C. (2001) 'Persistence pays off: working with "hard to reach" parents', in M. Whalley and the Pen Green Centre Team, *Involving Parents in their Children's Learning*. London: Paul Chapman Publishing.

Athey. C. (2007) *Extending Thought in Young Children: A Parent–Teacher Partnership*, 2nd edn. London: Sage.

Baz, P., Begun, L., Chia, K., Mason, G., Nutbrown, C. and Wragg, L. (1997) 'Working bilingually with families', in C. Nutbrown and P. Hannon (eds), *Preparing for Early Literacy Education with Parents: A Professional Development Manual*. Nottingham/Sheffield: NES Arnold/University of Sheffield, School of Education.

Delaney, P. (1997) 'A study of the provision for literacy development in early childhood education in Northern Ireland'. Unpublished M.Ed. dissertation, University of Sheffield, School of Education.

DES (1990) *Starting with Quality: Report of the Committee of Inquiry into the Quality of Educational Experience Offered to Three and Four Year Olds*. London: HMSO.

Draper, L. and Duffy, B. (2001) 'Working with parents', in G. Pugh (ed.), *Contemporary Issues in the Early Years: Working Collaboratively for Children*. London: Paul Chapman Publishing.

Fagan, W.T. (2000) 'Family literacy: fives steps to success', *Literacy Today*, 24: 26.

Firth, R. (1997) 'Brunswick Primary School "Parents' in Partnership" Project', in C. Nutbrown and P. Hannon (eds), *Preparing for Early Literacy Education with Parents: A Professional Development Manual*. Nottingham/Sheffield: NES Arnold/University of Sheffield, School of Education.

Hirst, K. (1998) 'Pre-school literacy experiences of children in Punjabi, Urdu and Gujerati speaking families in England', *British Educational Research Journal*, 24(4):.415–29.

Hurst, V. and Joseph, J. (eds) (2003) *Supporting Early Learning: The Way Forward*. Buckingham: Open University Press.

Karran, S. (2003) '"Auntie-Ji, please come and join us, just for an hour." The role of the bilingual education assistant in working with parents with little confidence', in J. Devereaux and L. Miller (eds), *Working with Children in the Early Years*. London: David Fulton/Open University.

Nutbrown, C. (2011) *Threads of Thinking: Schemas and Young Children Learning* 4th edn. London: Sage.

Nutbrown, C. and Carter, C. (2010) 'Watching and Listening: The tools of assessment', in G. Pugh and B. Duffy (2010) (eds) *Contemporary Issues in the Early Years*, 5th edn. London: Sage.

Nutbrown, C. and Hannon, P. (eds) (1997) *Preparing for Early Literacy Education with Parents: A Professional Development Manual*. Sheffield/Nottingham: NES Arnold/ University of Sheffield REAL Project.

Nutbrown, C., Hannon, P. and Collier, S. (1996) *Early Literacy Education with Parents: A Framework for Practice*. (Video.) Sheffield: The REAL Project/University of Sheffield, Sheffield University Television.

Nutbrown, C., Hannon, P. and Morgan, A. (2005) *Early Literacy Work with Parents: Policy, Practice and Research*. London: Sage.

Parker, C. (2002) 'Working with families on curriculum: developing shared understandings of children's mark making', in C. Nutbrown (ed.), *Research Studies in Early Childhood Education*. Stoke-on-Trent: Trentham.

Preece, V. (1999) 'Bridging the gap: investigating parents' and teachers' perceptions on parental involvement in the development of literacy'. Unpublished Ed. dissertation, University of Sheffield, School of Education.

Qualifications and Curriculum Authority (QCA) (2000) *Curriculum Guidance for the Foundation Stage*. London: QCA.

Rigo-Toth, R. and Ure, C. (2000) 'Evaluating literacy in the preschool a review of Hannon's ORIM framework', *International Journal of Learning*, 7

Roberts, R. (ed.) (2001) *PEEP Voices: A Five Year Diary*. Oxford: PEEP.

Siraj-Blatchford, I. (1994) *The Early Years: Laying the Foundations for Racial Equality*. Stoke-on-Trent: Trentham Books.

Turnbull, C. (1998) 'How valuable is the ORIM framework as a tool for nursery nurses developing the early literacy skills of preschool children?' Unpublished Ed. dissertation, University of Sheffield, School of Education.

Vygotsky, L. S. (1978) *Mind in Society*. Cambridge, MA: Harvard University Press.

Whalley, M. and the Pen Green Centre Team (1997) *Involving Parents in their Children's Learning*. London: Paul Chapman Publishing.

parental involvement

> *Persona Dolls are specially created dolls (about the size of a toddler) that are used to tell stories that raise issues of equality, promote talk and discussion of personal thoughts and feelings, and teach about difference. The dolls are designed to represent a range of cultures and family backgrounds.*

Anti-bias Persona Dolls emanate from the work of Derman-Sparkes in the US as part of the work of the Anti-Bias Curriculum Task Force. The dolls are used by practitioners to create and tell stories which challenge children to think about issues of equality in the lives of young children. The dolls are given personalities, with details of their names, birthday, family members, life history, geographical and cultural background. The dolls are of child-like size and practitioners who use them employ strategies to help the children see the dolls as part of the group. These Persona Dolls are not toys, but 'brought' to the group by the practitioner who might tell a story about the doll or ask the children to help the doll deal with something that has happened to him or her. The dolls are obtainable commercially, but could be made by people with the skills and knowledge to ensure that they and their clothes are culturally appropriate and that any particular physical features are accurate.

Brown suggests that dolls can be introduced as follows:

> One could be told about a particular doll – let's call her Beverley. She is four years old, loves riding her bike, painting and looking at books. She can't hear very well so everyone in her family uses sign language when they talk to her. Sometimes children tease her and then she feels sad. She lives with her black mum who is a doctor, her white dad who is a nursery school teacher, her sisters, Pam who is 7 and Irene who is 9 years old. They live in a flat which is right next to a park. Beverley has just started going to the same school as her sisters … The children can be encouraged to tell their own stories about the dolls and their families. (Brown, 1998: 101)

With the doll in the group setting, children become involved in the stories of their lives and engage in the issues which affect them (being teased, being called names, wearing glasses, and so on) and become involved in deciding how, in the group, the children could help to make things fairer and more positive for the doll. The dolls are an aid to helping children learn about discrimination, fairness and social justice issues

There are several areas for research, not least in the effectiveness of the strategy of using Persona Dolls to help children understand discrimination and to extend their knowledge of lives of people who are different from them. Studies are needed of the effectiveness of professional development for practitioners who use the dolls and how work with the dolls can be sustained and incorporated into the curriculum and pedagogy of the setting.

Derman-Sparkes and Taus (1989) suggest that children can begin to reach an understanding of diversity through storytelling. They write:

> Between the ages of two and five years old, children are forming self-identities and building social interaction skills. At the same time, they are becoming aware of and curious about gender, race, ethnicity and disabilities. Gradually young children begin to figure out how they are alike and how they are different from other people, and how they feel about those differences. (1989: 43)

CITY OF PHOENIX HEAD START PERSONA DOLLS PROJECT

The City of Phoenix Head Start Persona Dolls Project (Colunga, 2003) began in 1994 and included a training programme for Head Start teachers, using dolls with different types of hair, skin tone, abilities, ages and clothing. The dolls were given their own unique identities that included a name, family, likes and dislikes, cultural identity and idiosyncratic personal details (as all children have). The teachers used the dolls to tell stories about them, the things that happened to them, difficulties they encountered, their troubles and pleasures. Those who used the dolls most successfully integrated them into their classroom practice throughout the year – weaving stories of the dolls to link with children's experiences and to introduce them to new ideas and experiences of others.

PERSONA DOLLS IN HIGHER EDUCATION

Farmer, (2002) used Persona Dolls with a mixed aged group (from 17 to 50) of 25 BTEC Early Years students studying a Values and Personal

Table 3 Family structure and lifestyles of the Persona Dolls

Name of doll	Family structure	Occupation classification (NS – SEC)		Housing
Ayisha	Nuclear, 3 children	Accountant and teacher	1.2	House
Emily	Nuclear, 2 children	Previously farming	4.	4 bedroom large house
Emma	Nuclear, 3 children	Not stated		3 bedroom bungalow
Jurema	Nuclear, 3 children	Doctor and house husband	1.2	4 bedroom detached
Josh	Nuclear, 3 children	International company–no level		Nice house near beach
Kim	Nuclear, 2 children	Not stated		House
Laura	Nuclear, 2 children	Both parents work in the media	2	Large semi-detached
Mayra	Nuclear, 3 children	Doctor and Vet	1.2	Not stated
Rosa-May	Nuclear, 3 children	Nurse and fire-fighter	2 2	Not stated
Santinia	Extended + 1 child	Not stated		Caravan/cottage
Sita	Nuclear, 3 children	Not stated		Not stated

Note: (NS – SEC): National Statistics Socio-economic Classifications.
Source: Farmer (2002: 149).

Development module at a college of further education. Each doll was given a family background as summarised in Table 3.

The profiles of the dolls were created to represent a range of families, traditions, cultures and circumstances as the examples in Figure 6 show.

The use of the dolls had a great impact on the students' understanding of their own beliefs, values and prejudices, and of the assumption they held about others who were different from themselves. Farmer writes:

> In challenging the 'truths' of class, age, status, race, ethnicity, gender, ability or language superiority, I intended the students to develop understanding and tolerance for diversity. I would not presume to suggest that their attitudes, long-held prejudices or assumptions have been altered ... But ...

21 of the 25 students were able to relate to at least one area of diversity, address their own concerns and show awareness of how intolerance, discrimination and prejudice affects everyone. (2002: 154)

Jumera is English, 3½ years old, youngest of three. Mother, a doctor, is from Angola. Father, a 'house husband'. Holiday – a first visit to Angola. Doll has two outfits, for England and for Africa.

Mayra is Thai, with an English mother, Thai father, 3 years old, with an older and a younger brother. The family has recently arrived from Thailand. Mayra likes painting, poetry, stories and playing with dolls.

Santinia is 5 years old, English, and her parents are Spanish. They live with her grandparents and travel as a group of six caravans. Liti her rag doll is carried in a bag. She enjoys drawing and painting, as she has no television in the caravan.

Figure 6   *Profiles of the dolls*
Source: (Farmer 2002: 148).

REFERENCES AND INDICATIVE FURTHER READING

Brown, B. (1998) *Unlearning Discrimination in the Early Years*. Stoke-in-Trent: Trentham.

Brown, B. (2001) *Combating Discrimination Persona Dolls in Action*. Stoke-on-Trent: Trentham.

Colunga, C. (2003) *City of Phoenix Head Start Persona Dolls Project*. Available at: www.peopleofeverystripe.us.html

Derman-Sparkes, L. and the ABC Task Force (1989) *Anti-bias Curriculum: Tools for Empowering Young Children*. Washington, DC: National Association for the Education of Young Children.

Derman-Sparkes, L. and Taus, K. (1989) 'We're different … And we're friends!', *Scholastic Children Today*, 4(3):43–6, 60.

Farmer, G. (2002) 'Dolls with stories to tell: understanding bias and diversity', in C. Nutbrown (ed.), *Research Studies in Early Childhood Education*. Stoke-on Trent: Trentham.

Siraj-Blatchford, I. (1994) *The Early Years: Laying the Foundations for Racial Equality*. Stoke-on-Trent: Trentham.

Taus, K. (2000) *The Powers of Persona Dolls*. Available at: www.peopleofeverystripe.com/page9.html

Whitney, T. (1999) *Kids Like Us. Using Persona Dolls in the Classroom*. St Paul, MN: Redleaf Press.

> *Play in childhood is an exceedingly complex phenomenon. It is an activity which combines into a single whole, very different strands of thought and experience. Many of these persist in adult life. (Lowenfeld, 1935)*

As is it commonly understood in early childhood education and care, play is a central component of children's experiences and a key means by which they learn. Defining play is problematic, though the word 'play' is used liberally and with the assumption that its meaning is understood. Several famous pioneers of early childhood education – Montessori, Steiner, Froebel, Isaacs, the McMillan sisters – included play as central to their work in developing nursery and kindergarten curricula. Play has, in turn, been heralded as the essential means through which children learn and castigated and sidelined in favour of ensuring that young children should 'work' in school. In the introduction to their book *Structuring Play in the Early Years at School* Manning and Sharp (1977: 7) explain the purpose of the project on which they report:

> The idea of the project first arose because of the difficulties which many teachers were experiencing in using play in the classroom. Although accepting that children learn and develop through play and that play is a motivating force for children's learning, many teachers are pressurised by the very full first school curriculum and large classes to neglect play as a means of teaching. They leave children to play on their own. In addition, many parents' expectations are that children will 'work' when they come to school, not 'play'.

Over 30 years later many teachers continue to struggle to 'fit' play into their pedagogic repertoire and, though play is now reinstated in terms of the early years, some practitioners still lack the necessary skills and confidence to support children's play with children over five years old. The British Educational Research Association (BERA) reviewed research on early years pedagogy, curriculum and adult roles. Of play the review stated:

Several key studies have provided an evidence base on the quality of play, its educational benefits, and the pedagogy of play, in the contexts of pre-school and school settings (Tizard et al 1975, Sylva et al 1980, Wood et al 1980, Meadows and Cashdan, 1988; Hutt et al 1989, Bennett and Kell, 1989, Cleave and Brown, 1991; Bennett et al 1997). Most of these studies did not focus specifically on play, but on broader curriculum and peda-gogical processes, of which play was an integral part. Their findings were critical of the quality of play, the dislocation between rhetoric and reality of play; the extent to which play and learning were linked; the role of the adults in children's play, and how play was utilised towards educational outcomes. The consistent picture to emerge from these studies is that play in practice has been limited in frequency, duration and quality, with teach-ers and other adults too often adopting a reactive 'watching and waiting' approach. (BERA EYSIG,2003: 14)

While research evidence is inconclusive, the propensity of children the world over to play and the perceived benefits of play to children's holis-tic development provide a strong case for the professional exploration of the role of play in supporting children's well-being, development and learning.

In recent years more attention has been paid to children from birth to three and their play, too, is an issue for many practitioners. Manning-Morton and Thorp (2004) examine the importance of play for children under three years of age and identify the crucial role for adults in such play by supporting and developing play experiences. Play is seen in rela-tion to all aspects of a child's day, integral to and part of an holistic approach to early education and care for very young children.

Research continues to focus on definitions of play, children's roles and interests in play and how play is supported in various forms of early years provision in a variety of international contexts. These themes con-tinue to form the research agenda and, internationally, rich examples of children's play are still necessary. Questions about the efficacy of play as a pedagogical tool remain and successive governments show varied com-mitment to early years and school curriculum in relation to play. The implementation of the National Literacy and National Numeracy strate-gies, for example, promoted the importance of the basic skills and threatened play. Teachers became anxious that standards were raised at a cost and play was sidelined (and in some cases eliminated). Christmas (2005) asked the teachers and other staff in her small village school for their views on play, she found that while people generally thought it was 'OK to play' – worries over the play–work balance remained.

ZOE AND THE WATER WHEEL

Zoe, aged 4 years, was playing in the water trough in the nursery. She was experimenting with a jug and water wheel, spending a considerable time filling the jug, pouring the water over the wheel and watching it turn. She poured water at different speeds, and from different heights. Her teacher watched and eventually asked: 'Can you tell me what is happening?' Zoe looked at her and began her explanation: 'The wheel doesn't like to get wet, so it runs fast to get away from the water. When all the water is gone, it stays still again!'. Zoe knew that the water made the wheel turn but ascribed attributes of thought and feeling to the wheel. (Nutbrown, 2011: 3)

The Early Years Foundation Stage (EYFS) says this about play in early years settings:

Play and Exploration is one of the commitments to the EYFS principle of Learning and Development. The explanation of the commitment includes learning through experience, adult involvement and plenty of space and time to play outdoors and indoors. Practitioners need to ensure effective practice and reflection, overcoming time constraints and balancing creative learning with planning for the group.

Adult involvement

- Play comes naturally and spontaneously to most children, though some need adult support.
- Practitioners plan and resource a challenging environment where children's play can be supported and extended.
- Practitioners can extend and develop children's language and communication in their play through sensitive observation and appropriate intervention.
- Practitioners always intervene in play if it is racist, sexist or in any way offensive, unsafe, violent or bullying.

Contexts for learning

- Children need plenty of space and time to play, both outdoors and indoors.
- Children who are allowed to play with resources and equipment before using them to solve a problem are more likely to solve the problem successfully.

- Making dens and dressing-up are an integral part of children's play and they don't require expensive resources.
- Role-play areas allow children to take on and rehearse new and familiar roles. (DCSF, 2008: 29)

Themes of children's play are often influenced by their experiences – either first-hand or secondary experiences such as gleaned from television or stories. The practices of practitioners faced with war and gun play vary from 'zero tolerance' to a strategy of embracing and seeking to enhance the play. Holland (2003) argues that war, weapon and superhero play properly supported with sensitive adult guidance, can be generally positive experiences of children and practitioners, resulting in imaginative play and social development. Hyder (2004) explores the importance of play for young refugee children's development. She considers the implications of war and conflict on young children and notes how opportunities for play are often denied them. Hyder's work with young refugee children is set in the context of the United Nations Convention on the Rights of the Child and she argues that play is a healing experience for young children affected by war and conflict.

REFERENCES AND INDICATIVE FURTHER READING

Bennett, N. and Kell, J. (1989) *A Good Start? Four Year Olds in Infant Schools.* Oxford: Blackwell.

Bennett, N., Wood, E. and Rogers, S. (1997) *Teaching through Play: Teachers Thinking and Classroom Practice.* Buckingham: Open University Press.

British Educational Research Association Early Years Special Interest Group (BERA EYSIG) (2003) *Early Years Research: Pedagogy, Curriculum and Adult Roles, Training and Professionalism.* Nottingham: BERA.

Christmas, J. (2005) 'Is it OK to play?', in K. Horst and C. Nutbrown (eds), *Perspectives on Early Education: Essays in Contemporary Research.* Stoke-on-Trent: Trentham.

Cleave, S. and Brown, S. (1991) *Early to School: Four Year Olds in Infant Classes.* Slough: NFER/Nelson.

DCSF (2008) *Statutory Framework for the Early Years Foundation Stage Setting the Standards for Learning, Development and Care for Children from Birth to Five.* London: HMSO.

Holland, P. (2003) *We Don't Play with Guns Here.* Buckingham: Open University Press.

Hutt, S.J., Tyler, S., Hutt, C. and Christopherson, H. (1989) *Play, Exploration and Learning: A Natural History of the Preschool.* London: Routledge.

Hyder, T. (2004) *War, Conflict and Play.* Buckingham: Open University Press.

Jenkinson, S. (2001) *The Genius of Play: Celebrating the Spirit of Childhood.* Stroud: Hawthorn Press.

Lowenfeld, M. (1935) *Play in Childhood.* London: Gollanz.

play

Manning, K. and Sharp, A. (1977) *Structuring Play in the Early Years at School*. London: Ward Lock Educational.

Manning-Morton, J. and Thorp, M. (2004) *Key Times for Play*. Buckingham: Open University Press.

Meadows, S. and Cashdan, A. (1988) *Helping Children Learn: Contributions to a Cognitive Curriculum*. London: David Fulton.

Moyles, J. (ed.) (1994) *The Excellence of Play*. Buckingham: Open University Press.

Nutbrown, C. (2011) *Threads of Thinking: Schemas and Young Children Learning*, 4th edn. London: Sage.

Sutton-Smith, B. (1997) *The Ambiguity of Play*. Cambridge, MA: Harvard University Press.

Sylva, K., Roy, C. and Painter, M. (1980) *Child Watching at Playgroup and Nursery*. London: Grant McIntyre.

Tizard, B., Phelps, J. and Plewis, I. (1975) 'Play in preschool centres: play measures and their relation to age, sex and IQ', *Journal of Child Psychology and Psychiatry*, 17: 251–62.

Wood, D., McMahon, L. and Cranstoun, Y. (1980) *Working with Under Fives*. London: Grant McIntyre.

Wood, L. and Bennett, N. (1997) 'The rhetoric and reality of play: teachers' thinking and classroom practice', *Early Years*, 17(2): 22–7.

quality

> *'Quality' has evolved as the term used to describe merits of provision and practices in early childhood education and care. It is a term that evades precise definition and depends much on the values, philosophies and practices of those involved.*

The issue of what is 'good' for children in the early years of their organised education is one that impinges on many factors and which has pervaded policy and practice in modern times. The extent to which early childhood education is 'good' for children, the forms of early years practice and types of provision which are most 'effective', and the activities in settings which are 'best practice' in extending children's holistic development are all questions which, together, inform discussion about the 'quality' of provision for young children – and, more recently, for their families too. The 'quality' discussion centres around what is offered to young children, where it is offered, by whom and to what effect. Definitions of 'high' or 'good' quality, or of 'best practice' and beliefs about how to achieve such quality in providing for children's early education and care, determine many things, such as: the qualifications of staff who work with young children; the nature of equipment; the premises and physical surroundings and facilities; the nature of the curriculum; the pedagogical practices – to name but a few. Quality is a multifaceted concept and is, necessarily, culturally determined. It is impossible (and probably undesirable) to produce a single 'blueprint' for quality in early childhood education and care and apply it – universally – in everyday education settings throughout the world. Needs, opportunities, priorities and individual choices vary, and if early childhood settings are to be of good quality then one factor which determines its worth is the extent to which the provision is meaningful and appropriate to those who use it.

Discussion in the early childhood literature on quality suggests that the many factors which contribute to quality provision – which is 'good' for children – include:

119

- the involvement of parents;
- liaison between a range of agencies and sectors;
- the rights and needs of the children; environment, equipment and resources;
- health, safety and protection;
- curriculum and learning opportunities;
- roles of professionals and responsible adults;
- management and organisation;
- observation, assessment and recording achievement;
- evaluation and review of provision.

National standards exist to ensure that provision meets agreed levels of care, though these alone do not necessarily constitute the highest quality of provision that it is possible to achieve. In recent years new forms of provision have been developed, such as Children's Centres which have been flagged as the modern pioneers of good practice and quality provision. One feature of such Centres is the multifaceted nature of provision which combines a range of services under one umbrella of service for children and their families. Such coordinated provision is a key aim of Sure Start.

The many factors to be considered in developing and defining quality can be seen as touchstones for policies and practices in early childhood provision, and can act as signposts to achieving and monitoring quality. Statements of principle which overarch all provision for young children need to be considered, discussed, adopted, adapted, applied and evaluated on a regular basis – this process of perpetual reflection in itself constituting an element of quality provision.

Many systems exist for the monitoring of quality provided by settings and services. Inspection frameworks are clear and transparent and serve to provide a form of quality assurance as measured against agreed and published standards and criteria. However, those standards and frameworks alone do not define the essence of quality as informed by research as it is continually developed in practice.

Six factors could be considered as starting points for quality and form a clear research agenda:

- coordination of services;
- parents are the prime educators of their children;
- consistency, continuity and progression in pedagogy;
- equality of opportunity;

- acting in the best interests of children;
- respect.

COORDINATION OF SERVICES

Before formal schooling begins, young children receive many early experiences of education and care in a range of settings, and different settings and services may be the responsibility of different government departments, or private, voluntary or other community groups. Agencies responsible for young children are now required to collaborate in providing for them and Sure Start Children's Centre programmes and the Children Act 2005 made for 'joined up' services for children and their families – the 'one stop shop' appears to be one element which can contribute to quality provision in the early twenty-first century. Quality provision for young children is enhanced when:

- information is available to parents about what kinds of provision are available for children;
- multiprofessional and interagency training and professional development are available for people who work with and need to know more about young children and their learning;
- policy and practices in terms of transition of children from one setting to another are coherent and take account of the needs and family backgrounds of the children and their parents;
- networks of provision are established to facilitate the sharing of understanding about provision for children's needs and their learning.

For more information see: (DCSF, 2008; Pugh and Duffy, 2010)

PARENTS ARE THE PRIME EDUCATORS OF THEIR CHILDREN

Early childhood educators working in home or group settings are increasingly aware of the central role of children's parents in their living and learning. Parents are responsible for their children's experiences and so, two-way dialogue, consultation and information sharing need to be an aim of early education. Educators in all early childhood education and care settings need to develop positive relationships with parents which reflect the primary role of parents in their children's lives, and clear policies on parental involvement can help to develop frameworks for the involvement of all parents.

For more information see: (Draper and Duffy, 2001; Nutbrown and Hannon, 2005; Whalley, 1997)

CONSISTENCY, CONTINUITY AND PROGRESSION IN PEDAGOGY

Children have developing minds and bodies which need to be nurtured and protected as they grow towards independence. Consistency of care is important, children feel secure when they know (for example) who is looking after them, who their teacher is, who will be at playgroup, who will put them to bed. Children need opportunities to develop consistent relationships with other children and with adults, developing confidence in themselves and trust in others.

Continuity of care and education is crucial in the early years of childhood, and increasingly early education centres for children under three are attending to the need to have a Key Person who takes major responsibility for all aspects of their learning and development and care routines in the group settings (Elfer et al., 2003; Page, 2005; Page and Nutbrown, 2008). Nutbrown (2011) discusses the importance of continuity in curriculum terms, both in relation to content and structure (or form) of children's thinking, and the importance of children having space and opportunity to construct their own continuities of learning as well as experiencing teacher-constructed-or controlled continuity.

The progression of individual children, their development and growth needs to be monitored and some dialogue between parents and other educators concerned with the child needs to take place if children move from one setting to another. Children's learning and development can be supported and extended by planned learning opportunities, according to their needs.

For more information see: (DCSF, 2008; Goldschmied and Jackson, 1994; Nutbrown, 2006)

EQUALITY OF OPPORTUNITY

The principle of equality for all children and families is a responsibility at national, local, community, group and individual levels. Those responsible for planning services need to ensure that facilities are available, accessible and appropriate for the needs of all members of the community – however young. Services and facilities for children who are disabled should be available to all children in their local communities, and education settings for all young children need to be critically aware of and challenging towards the racist and sexist practices which marginalise, exclude and discriminate against some families. In striving for equality, educators must ask themselves questions about their practice with children and their parents. On the UK context, Nutbrown posed a number of questions:

> Is the important role of all parents acknowledged? Do all parents believe that the workers who spend time with their children want them as parents to be involved? Are black parents, single parents, parents living in extreme poverty, parents who are disabled, parents who complain and ask questions, parents of children with special educational needs, are they all involved in the life and developments within the group setting as far as they wish to be? Or do educators select in some ways the parents who they feel will be 'best' fitted for the roles they have created for them? (Nutbrown, 1996: 139)

Where children are concerned, educators need to examine their interactions with *all* the children under their care. As Nutbrown (1996: 54) has it:

> Respectful educators will strive to afford every child equality of opportunity. Not just those who are easy to work with, obliging, endearing, clean, pretty, articulate, capable, but every child – respecting them for who they are, respecting their language, their culture, their history, their family, their abilities, their needs, their name, their ways and their very essence. This means understanding children's needs and building on their abilities.

For more information see: (Brooker, 2005; Brown, 1998; Siraj-Blatchford, 1994)

ACTING IN THE BEST INTERESTS OF CHILDREN

Any form of provision for young children should consider what practices are actually in the best interests of children. Practices and routines are sometimes adopted because they suit the adults, but stock-taking of rationale for practices can identify whether what happens is terms of routines, curriculum, assessment and a range of activities within those elements of work, are done in ways which are best for the children or because they may the working day slightly easier for adults. Questions of quality, what is good and bad for children or what is best for children in the early stages of learning are constant matters for debate, but some factors can perhaps be undisputed. That it is in children's best interests that the building in which they learn is safe, that they are free from danger of abduction or health risks, for example are not issues for debate. The UN Convention on the rights of children to *survival, development, protection* and *participation* in their societies are paramount, and clearly there are implications here for early childhood settings and services. Yet there are many aspects of quality which are more contestable: *what* children 'should' learn; *how* they 'should' be taught; *when* and *how* such learning 'should' be assessed, to name but a few. Responses to such issues need to be developed in an international context, with appropriate consideration of culture, heritage, expectations, legislation and rights.

RESPECT

It can be argued that achieving the best for young children is a matter of adopting a respectful and inclusive attitude to all aspects of provision and practice. A respectful disposition to young children and their families enables educators to work for what is best for young children. When advocates of respectful provision are accused of being 'idealistic' or of 'romanticising' early childhood, their meaning is misunderstood. Respect is not about 'being nice'. It is about being clear, honest, courteous, diligent and consistent. Respect for children will enable adults to fulfil their responsibilities towards children. Respect for children is a disposition which enables adults who work with young children to fulfil their responsibilities, enabling re-creation where children discover and make and play and grow.

For more information see: (Nutbrown, 1998; DES/Sure Start, 2003; Rinaldi, 1999)

Early childhood practice and research is rich with examples of high quality provision for young children, in the context of the above. Quality, too, is also a personal construct – it lies 'in the eye of the beholder'. This section therefore includes, not examples *of* 'quality' but commentaries on – or essentials *for* quality.

The REPEY (Researching Effective Pedagogy in the Early Years) study (Siraj Blatchford et al., 2002) sought to identify how the quality characteristics highlights in the project worked in practice to impact positively on children's learning. REPEY findings indicated that three things were important: adult and child *involvement, cognitive engagement,* and *instruction* (such as modelling, demonstration, explanation and questioning). REPEY highlights the complex nature of achieving quality in teaching and learning.

The Effective Provision of Pre-school Education (EPPE) study has reported on factors – in a range of pre-school settings – which impact on children's achievement (Sammons et al., 2002a; Sammons et al., 2002b; Siraj-Blatchford et al., 2002). It could be described as the largest and most intensive scrutiny of quality and the impact of quality in early childhood settings in the UK. The study has helped to identify the aspects of pre-school provision which positively impact on children's learning and development in the early years.

For more information see: (DFES/DOH, 2004; UN, 1989)

REFERENCES AND INDICATIVE FURTHER READING

Abbott, L. and Langston, A. (2005) *Birth to Three Matters: Supporting the Framework of Effective Practice*. Buckingham: Open University Press.

Anning, A., Cullen, J. and Fleer, M. (eds) (2004) *Early Childhood Education: Society and Culture*. London: Sage.

Bertram, A. and Pascal, C. (2000) *Early Excellence Centres. Developing High-quality Integrated Early Years Services First Findings, Autumn 1999*. London: DfEE.

Brooker, L. (2005) 'Learning to be a child: cultural diversity and early years ideology', in N. Yelland, (ed.), *Critical Issues in Early Childhood Education*. Buckingham: Open University Press.

Brown, B. (1998) *Unlearning Discrimination in the Early Years*. Stoke-on-Trent: Trentham.

Dalhberg, G., Moss, P. and Pence, A. (1999) *Beyond Quality in Early Childhood Education and Care: Postmodern Perspectives*. London: Falmer Press.

DCSF (2008) *Statutory Framework for the Early Years Foundation Stage Setting the Standards for Learning, Development and Care for Children from Birth to Five*. London: HMSO.

Department for Education and Skills (DfES) and Department of Health (DoH) (2004) *National Service Framework for Children, young People and Maternity Service: Executive Summary*. London: HMSO.

DES (1991) *Starting with Quality: Report of the Committee of Inquiry into the Quality of Educational Experience Offered to 3- and 4-Year-Olds*. (Rumbold Report.) London: HMSO.

DES/Sure Start (2003) *Sure Start: Introduction 1 December 2003*. Available at: www.surestart.gov.uk Department of Work and Pensions/Department for Education and Skills, PO Box 5050, Sherwood Park, Annesley, Nottingham, NG15 0DJ.

DfES (2001) *National Standards for Under Eights' Day Care and Childminding*. London: DfES Publications.

DfES/QCA (2000) *Curriculum Guidance for the Foundation Stage*. London: DfES Publications.

Draper, L. and Duffy, B. (2001) 'Working with parents', in G. Pugh (ed.), *Contemporary Issues in the Early Years: Working Collaboratively for Children*. London: Paul Chapman Publishing.

Drummond, M.J. (1999) 'The Steiner Schools', paper presented at 'Visions and Choices in Partnership' conference, University of London, 12 October.

Early Childhood Education Forum (1998) *Quality in Diversity in Early Learning*. London: National Children's Bureau.

Elfer, P., Goldschmied, E. and Selleck, D. (2003) *Key Persons in the Nursery: Building Relationships for Quality Provision*. London: David Fulton.

Goldschmied, E. and Jackson, S. (1994) *People Under Three: Young Children in Day Care*. London: Routledge.

Munton, A.G. and Mooney, A. (1997) 'Enhancing quality in day care: theories of organisational change', *Early Years*. 18(1). 47–52.

Nutbrown, C. (1996) *Respectful Educators: Capable Learners: Children's Rights in the Early Years*. London: Paul Chapman Publishing.

Nutbrown, C. (1998) *The Lore and Language of Early Education*. Sheffield: USDE.

Nutbrown, C. (2011) *Threads of Thinking: Schemas and Young Children Learning*, 4th edn. London: Sage.

Nutbrown, C. and Hannon, P. (eds) (1997) *Preparing for Early Literacy Education with Parents: A Professional Development Manual*. Sheffield/Nottingham: NES Arnold/ University of Sheffield REAL Project.

Nutbrown, C., Hannon, P. and Morgan, A. (2005) *Early Literacy Work with Families: Research, Policy and Practice*. London: Sage.

Nutbrown, C. and Carter, C. (2010) 'Watching and Listening: the Tools of Assessment', in G. Pugh and B. Duffy (2006) (eds), *Contemporary issues in the Early Years*, 5th edn. London: Sage.

OECD (2001) *Starting Strong: Early Childhood Education and Care*. Paris: OECD.

Page, J. (2005) 'Working with children under three: the perspectives of three UK academics', in K. Hirst and C. Nutbrown (eds), *Perspectives on Early Childhood Education: Essays in Contemporary Research*. Stoke-on-Trent: Trentham.

Page, J. and Nutbrown, C. (2008) 'How amazing: learning and development in under threes', *Nursery World*, 109 (4146): 24–5.

Pugh, G. (ed.) (2001) *Contemporary Issues in the Early Years: Working Collaboratively for Children*, 3rd edn. London: Paul Chapman Publishing.

Pugh, G. and Duffy, B. (2010) (eds) (5th edn) *Contemporary Issues in the Early Years: Working Collaboratively for Children*. London: Sage.

Rinaldi, C. (1999) 'The pedagogy of listening', paper given at the Reggio Emilia Conference, Reggio Emilia, Italy, 28 April.

Sammons, P., Sylva, K., Melhuish, E., Siraj-Blatchford, I., Taggart, B. and Elliott, K. (2002a) *EPPE Technical Paper 8a – Measuring the Impact of Pre-school on Children's Cognitive Progress over the Pre-school Period*. London: Institute of Education.

Sammons, P., Sylva, K., Melhuish, E., Siraj-Blatchford, I., Taggart, B. and Elliott, K. (2002b) *EPPE Technical Paper 8b – Measuring the Impact of Pre-school on Children's Social/Behavioural Development over the Pre-school Period*. London: Institute of Education.

Siraj-Blatchford, I. (1994) *The Early Years: Laying the Foundations for Racial Equality*. Stoke on Trent: Trentham.

Siraj-Blatchford, I., Sylva, K. Muttock, S., Gildan, R. and Bell, D. (2002) *Researching Effective Pedagogy in the Early Years*. Research Report No. 356. London: Department of Education and Skills

United Nations (1989) *Convention on the Rights of the Child*. New York: United Nations.

Weinberger, J., Pickstone, C. and Hannon, P. (eds) (2005) *Learning from Sure Start: Working with Young Children and their Families*. Buckingham: Open University Press.

Whalley, M. and the Pen Green Centre Team (1997) *Involving Parents in their children's learning*. London: Paul Chapman Publishing.

> The 'Reggio Approach' refers to a set of pedagogical practices – developed in Reggio Emilia, Northern Italy – which is based on respect for childhood, children's rights and the development of communities of learners.

Reggio Emilia is a small town in Northern Italy where, in 1779 the Italian tricolour was 'born' thus giving the town an important place in Italian history. However, its claim to fame in early childhood terms is due to its international reputation for the quality of its provision for young children. Reggio Emilia is important to the world of early childhood because of its reputation for pioneering approaches to pre-school education. Since the 1960s, when the municipality of Reggio Emilia began setting up its distinctive form of pre-school education, the municipality has grown in international significance for the quality of provision it offers for young children. The 'Reggio Approach' has gained worldwide recognition, stimulated by international tours of the 'Hundred Languages of Childhood' exhibition which explains the approach and illustrates the processes and outcomes of its pedagogical approach through film and examples of children's work. Numerous visitors from around the globe have expressed great interest and respect for the work Reggio Emilia's Infant–Toddler (for children up to three years) and Pre-school (three to six years) Centres.

The Reggio Emilia approach to education has been developed through generations and evolved from a resolve to provide a better future for children following the years of occupation during the Second World War. The children who attend Reggio Emilia centres today are benefiting from the investment and commitment of their ancestors who created the foundations of an approach to pre-school pedagogy based on community and citizenship. Central to the Reggio Approach are carefully articulated theories of children as powerful, competent learners, as users of multiple forms of expression, of the need for educators to listen to children, and of the importance of the environment in facilitating children's learning. The whole environment is crucial in the Reggio system and, as Malaguzzi, founder of the Reggio Approach to pre-school education wrote:

We consider the environment to be an essential constituent element of any theoretical or political research in education. We hold to be equally valuable the rationality of the environment, its capacity for harmonious coexistence, and its highly important forms and functions. Moreover, we place enormous value on the role of the environment as a motivation and animating force in creating spaces for relations, options and emotional and cognitive situations that produce a sense of well-being and security. It has been said that the environment should act as a kind of aquarium, which reflects the ideas, ethics, attitudes and culture of the people who live in it. (Malaguzzi, 1996: 40)

Those pre-school environments are distinctive in character, with their open central *piazza* where children meet and play and share, their communal dining spaces where food is shared leisurely over conversation, mirrors and light spaces for exploring shape and space from different angles and the *atelier* (the art studio) where children work with the *atelierista* (the experienced and qualified artist on the staff). Colour and light are all important, as are documentary descriptions of the various projects children have carried out. The distinctiveness of the environments is difficult to describe but Leask's description of her son's infant–toddler centre gives a flavour:

Entering the school for the first time, the impact of my first impressions of so many years before came flooding back as we looked around a light open space filled with examples of children's work (but this was August – why weren't the walls bare?), written panels illustrated with photos, plants, a mix of small chairs and antique furniture, *bric-a-brac*, tiny beautiful treasures, delicate old objects and instruments, photos and examples of work that had obviously been there for many years – the sort of domestic archaeology layering that takes place over time in all our homes. (Leask, 2001: 43–4)

The Reggio Emilia approach to pedagogy in the early years raises many issues for research. Interested visitors often ask about the impact of such an approach on children's achievement and how the children cope with the transition from this form of learning experience to a more formal Italian state school system at six years old. But the questions which those from other countries and cultures might ask are broader and more specifically oriented towards the transferability of the Reggio Approach to their own settings. Would such an approach work in

Birmingham, or Sydney, or Dubai, or Bangkok? Peter Moss responds to this very question:

I see Reggio as an important, but not a generalisable experience. We cannot escape responsibility for making our own choices about early childhood by 'buying in' to a 'Reggio programme': for the choices we face are political and ethical, not between competing programmes or 'models of good practice'. At a time when in Britain a rhetoric of choice and diversity in the provision of early childhood services is matched by the application of a range of 'human technologies' ... intended to secure increasing standardisation in practice and purpose and to normalise our thinking and doing, one reason why Reggio is so important is that it reminds us that it is possible to think and do differently – that there are many different ways of working with young children, and indeed evaluating our work.

It is not that those in Reggio are right, and we in Britain are necessarily wrong. Rather, Reggio self-consciously *chooses* to work within a particular paradigm, aware that such a choice has certain consequences, In Britain on the other hand there is a lack of paradigmatic self-awareness, and instead a search for absolutes: the right way, best practice, quality, excellence. While we seek *the* answer which will enable us to foreclose, in Reggio they understand that even after 30 years or more, their work remains provisional, continually open to new conditions, perspectives, understandings and possibilities. (Moss, 2001: 125–6)

Abbott and Nutbrown (2001) identified a number of research issues stimulated by experiencing the work in Reggio Emilia pre-schools and infant–toddler centres including:

- the place of play;
- the role of listening in pedagogy;
- the roles of adults;
- parents' views and expectations;
- special educational needs;
- inclusion;
- architecture in pre-schools;
- dealing with children's responses to difficult issues.

Perhaps it is fair to say that the key research issues arising from Reggio Emilia which are global and transferable, have been identified by Carlina Rinaldo, a key figure in Reggio Emilia. She asked:

- What do we hope for children?
- What do we expect from children?
- What is the relationship between school and research?
- What is the relationship between school and community?
- What is the relationship between school, family and society?
- What is the relationship between school and life?
- Is school a preparation for, or part of, life?

A well-known example of Reggio practice is published as *The Fountains* (Reggio Children, 1995). This project involved children in the creation of *'un luna park degli uccellini'* (an 'amusement park for birds'). The children at 'La Vialetta' school spent many weeks in a collaborative project to create an amusement park for the birds in their pre-school garden. The introduction to the account of the project states that:

> It is only through a process of re-reading, reflection and revisiting that children are able to organise what they have learned from a single experience within a broader system of relations. These processes are individually and socially constructed, and herein lies the image of the child as an active constructor of his or her knowledge, which is one of the fundamental premises of the philosophy and practice that has come to be known as the 'Reggio Approach'. The Amusement Park for Birds is a wonderful example of school as a place where children are encouraged to reflect on an experience rather than simply have an experience, a context that stimulates children not only to observe but also to reflect on their observations. (Forman, in *Reggio Children*, 1995: 6)

This well-documented example of the Reggio Approach involved the children in collaborative, social construction of knowledges and understandings in a learning community. They revisited and revised their understanding day by day – rethinking and reconstructing their learning, in process, together.

Following a visit to the Reggio Emilia pre-schools, Parker (2001) developed her own practice of re-proposing to children their ideas and their language and inviting them to revise and rethink what they had done and said on previous occasions. In her account of the development of her practice with young bilingual children she concludes:

> Working through some of the ideas I brought back from Reggio leads me to suggest that:

- Reproposing children's talk enables children to expand on their theories and extend them. This process shows children that their ideas and thoughts are valued and can be shared and discussed. It reinforces their previous learning and develops them further. The children were confident in their use of new vocabulary and of tenses, and made connections.
- Revisiting children's mark-making results in similar outcomes. They can add to their work, review and alter theories. Their self-esteem develops and the adult has a starting point to develop the children's representational and cognitive skills. The added detail is significant.
- The processes of reproposing and revisiting children's theories has an impact on developing children's confidence in speaking English as an additional language.
- Working in a group together enables children to appreciate each other's achievements, learn from each other and develop their confidence.
- The value of focusing our attention on the children's concerns and interests is reinforced, allowing opportunities for spontaneous talk between children about those ideas and experiences that fascinate and inspire them.
- To enable practitioners to value children's theories through revisiting and reproposing requires some thought in practical terms of space, time, resources and staffing. All these issues have been considered in the Reggio Emilia settings and opportunities for extended study of a theory are provided for (Parker, 2001: 91).

The Sightlines Initiative is the UK reference point for the Reggio Children Network and was created to support creative thinking and to develop practice in the UK that promotes the growth of children's creative potential through:

- innovative projects;
- reflective practice;
- professional networking between artists and educators;
- advocacy, training and support.

REFERENCES AND INDICATIVE FURTHER READING

Abbott, L. and Nutbrown, C. (eds) (2001) *Experiencing Reggio Emilia: Implications for Preschool Provision*. Milton Keynes: Open University Press.
Edwards, G., Gandini, L. and Forman, G. (eds) (2001) *The Hundred Languages of Children – The Reggio Emilia Approach to Early Childhood Education*, 2nd edn. Norwood, NJ: Ablex.

reggio emilia approach

Johnson, R. (1999) 'Colonialism and cargo cults in early childhood education: does Reggio Emilia really exist?', *Contemporary Issues in Early Childhood*, 1(1): 61–77.

Leask, J. (2001) 'Sam's invisible extra gear – a parent's view', in L. Abbott and C. Nutbrown (eds), *Experiencing Reggio Emilia: Implications for Preschool Provision*. Milton Keynes: Open University Press.

Malaguzzi, L. (1996) 'The right to environment', in T. Filippini and V. Vecchi (eds), *The Hundred Languages of Children: The Exhibit*. Reggio Emilia: Reggio Children.

Malaguzzi, L. (1998) 'For an education based on relationships', *Young Children* November, 9–13.

Moss, P. (2001) 'The otherness of Reggio', in L. Abbott and C. Nutbrown (eds), *Experiencing Reggio Emilia: Implications for Preschool Provision*. Milton Keynes: Open University Press.

Parker, C. (2001) '"She's back!" The impact of my visit to Reggio Emilia on a group of 3- and 4-year olds', in L. Abbott and C. Nutbrown (eds), *Experiencing Reggio Emilia: Implications for Preschool Provision*. Milton Keynes: Open University Press.

Reggio Children (1995) *Le ontant da un progetto per la construzionedi un Luna Park degli uccellini [The Fountains: From a Project for the Construction of an Amusement Park for Birds]*. Reggio Emilia: Reggio Children.

Rofrano, F. (2000) 'A response to "Colonialism and Cargo Cults in early Childhood Education: does Reggio Emilia really exist?"', *Contemporary Issues in Early Childhood*, 1(2): 27–30.

Wright, S. (2000) 'Why Reggio Emilia doesn't exist: a response to Richard Johnson', *Contemporary Issues in Early Childhood*, 1(2): 227–30.

As generally understood in present early childhood pedagogy, a schema is 'a pattern of repeatable behaviour into which experiences are assimilated and that are gradually co-ordinated'.[6] The work of Athey (2007) made popular the incorporation of schemas into early childhood pedagogy in the learning of three to five year olds. More recent work has extended understanding of schematic learning to work with babies and toddlers.

There is no single or definitive definition of the term 'schema' and, although the current use of the term in early childhood education and care is that given above, earlier work (Piaget, 1953) identifies schemas as part of the study of cognitive structures of young children's developing minds. Athey (2007) gives a thorough explanation of the various roots and definitions of the term as derived from the work of Piaget (1969), Bartlett (1932) and Neisser (1976).

We now know more about the learning patterns (or schemas) of babies and how they might think and learn. Goldschmied (1989) demonstrates how babies, given safe, stimulating and supportive opportunities, will use their senses and their developing physical skills to learn about the objects they encounter. Babies, as they suck, handle and smell are in a world of discovery – they puzzle, enjoy social interactions with others and make attempts to communicate their feelings and their needs. Those who watch young babies see some of the early patterns of gazing and following with their eyes, and some of those basic patterns of behaviour (or schemas) are quite obvious to the observer. As babies suck and grasp they work on, develop and refine the early schematic behaviours which foster their early foundations of learning. Early patterns of behaviour seen in babies become more complex and more numerous, eventually being connected so that babies and young children coordinate their actions.

Toddlers work hard, collecting a pile of objects in the lap of their carer, walking to and fro, backwards and forwards, bringing one object at a time. They are working on a pattern of behaviour which has a consistent thread running through it. Their patterns of action and thought at this

---

[6]Athey (1990: 37).

point are related to the consistent back-and-forth movement. The early schemas of babies form the basis of the patterns of behaviour which children show between the ages of two and five years, and these in turn become established foundations of learning.

Athey (2007) maintains that children will notice elements in their environment, depending upon their interests at the time, and that they have their own intrinsic motivation which must be facilitated by materials and support from adults. Athey focused on how two to five year old children also work on particular patterns of behaviour, referring to each of these patterns as a schema and defining a schema as 'a repeatable pattern of behaviour into which experiences are assimilated and that are gradually co-ordinated' (Athey, 1990: 37). A number of patterns of behaviour were identified by Athey as part of the Froebel Early Education Project (which collected and analysed over 5,000 observations of 20 two- to five-year-olds over two years). These were named according to their characteristics. For example, a 'vertical schema' is so called because it relates to up-and-down movements. Athey discusses children's learning and development in terms of the following schemas:

- dynamic vertical;
- dynamic back and forth;
- dynamic circular;
- going over and under;
- going round a boundary;
- enveloping and containing space;
- going through a boundary.

The actions and marks related to these descriptions of movement can be identified in young children's drawing and mark-making, but Athey illustrates how such patterns can be represented in children's play, their thinking and their language. Athey argues that patterns pervade children's actions and speech as well as their mark-making. Detailed description and discussion on ways in which different patterns of learning can be represented through action, speech and mark-making are given by Athey, who further illustrates in theoretical and practical terms how forms of thought (schemas) once identified can be nourished with worthwhile content.

If a child is focusing on a particular schema related to 'roundness' we could say that she or he is working on a circular schema. The form is 'roundness' and the content can be anything which extends this form:

wheels, rotating machinery, rolling a ball, the spinning of planets! Similarly, a child interested in 'up and down ness' could be working on a vertical schema, The form is 'up and down'; related content can include using ladders, using the climbing frame, watching parascending or skydiving, riding in a lift or on an escalator. In the same way, if a child is interested in enclosing and enveloping schemas, the form is 'insideness' and related content may include wrapping presents, hatching chick eggs, *encroûte* cookery, mining and burrowing.

The main task for research is to provide further evidence of how children's schemas might be used to nourish children's thinking and how practitioners can develop their pedagogy to incorporate working with children's schemas.

Case studies are needed to demonstrate how current policy on curriculum in the early years provide for children's developmental patterns of learning. Educators can provide a more appropriate curriculum which matches the developmental levels and interests of the children by using their knowledge of schemas and their skills as observers to develop greater awareness of children's patterns of learning and understand more about children's predominant interests. Practitioner research of this kind, which illuminates the fine detail of individual children's learning can add to the bank of research studies which will, in turn, enable practitioners to reflect on their own strategies for helping young children to learn in developmentally appropriate ways.

Studies of children's schemas and how curriculum provides for such learning needs can show the relationship of theories of learning (such as Schematic Development) and current curriculum planning and pedagogy (Arnold, 2002).

There is space for further research which considers how assessment – through observation of children's schemas – can be incorporated into required assessment procedures and assist practitioners in making decisions about next steps in teaching and learning.

BELINDA'S ENCLOSING SCHEMA

Belinda was three years old and she seemed to be tuned into spotting or seeking out opportunities to enclose or be enclosed, and objects which enclosed. At home she enjoyed emptying and filling the washing machine, and in the garden and in the bath she filled numerous containers with water to the point that they overflowed. She and her mother built up a collection of tins and boxes that she enjoyed fitting inside one another in different combinations and she often enjoyed sitting inside cardboard boxes used to carry the shopping from the supermarket, sometimes pretending that the box was a car, bus, boat or rocket. Some of Belinda's favourite books contained stories of hiding or enclosing in one way or another, stories like *Where's Spot?* (Hill, 1980). At her sessional group Belinda particularly enjoyed playing in the house and hiding the farm animals inside the little wooden farm buildings. She dressed up and liked to play in the tunnel and hidey boxes outside.

Exploring her enveloping/containing schema, Belinda encountered much learning which linked with different areas of learning and experience. She learned about being with others and being apart, cooperating when equipment needed to be shared and dealing with her emotions when she wanted to be the only person to play in the house and was told to allow other children to play too. Opportunities at home and in the group enabled Belinda to explore her schema and develop her knowledge. The adults around her, sensitised to her interests, provided encouragement where a lack of knowledge may have led some adults to stop Belinda doing some of the things she found interesting.

All the adults who lived or worked with Belinda were able to support and extend her learning. She encountered situations which required her to develop and refine mathematical skills of collecting, sorting, selecting, counting, ordering, reordering, grading, categorising and placing. She puzzled over ideas of shape and size and how things fitted together. She asked questions such as: 'Why does the washing have to get covered in water before it is clean?', 'Why do we have to wrap the potatoes before they go in the oven?' and 'Why won't this one [big tin] fit inside this one here [smaller tin]?' Her mother extended her interest, and in doing so provided more connections between experiences, such as involving her in baking, washing, writing letters and posting them. They looked at holes and hiding places, talked about being inside a lift and packed the shopping into boxes in the supermarket. She began to learn more about space and place relationships, finding out about relative size. Belinda's mother acted on what she saw and what she understood.

key concepts in early childhood education and care

REFERENCES AND INDICATIVE FURTHER READING

Arnold, C. (2002) *Observing Harry.* Buckingham: Open University Press.

Athey, C. (2002) *Extending Thought in Young Children: A Parent–Teacher Partnership,* 2nd edn. London: Sage.

Athey, C. (2007) *Extending Thought in Young Children: A Parent–Teacher Partnership*, 2nd edn. London: Sage.

Bartlett, F.C. (1932) *Remembering: A Study of Experimental and Social Psychology*. Cambridge: Cambridge University Press.

Hill, E. (1980) *Where's Spot?* London: Heinemann.

Neisser, U. (1976) *Cognition and Reality*. San Francisco, CA: W.H. Freeman.

Nutbrown, C. (2011) *Threads of Thinking: Schemas and Young Children Learning*, 4th edn. London: Sage.

Piaget, J. (1953) *The Origin of Intelligence in the Child*. London: Routledge and Kegan Paul.

Piaget, J. (1969)*The Mechanisms of Perception*. London: Routledge and Kegan Paul.

schemas

> *The term sexuality is defined as 'a person's sexual orientation or preference'.[7] In the context of this discussion, 'sexualities' refers to the inclusion and non-marginalisation of lesbian, gay and bisexual parents and practitioners in early years settings.*

In the UK around 5 per cent of people identify themselves as lesbian, gay or bisexual (DoH, 2007) and, with changes in family characteristics and same-sex parenting, the likelihood of some settings having children who live with parents of the same sex is growing. For this reason, and because it is part of the work necessary in order to achieve fully inclusive practices, issues of sexuality are a concern in the early years. Issues of sexuality are important to consider in the early years because the children of same-sex parents, rarely encounter any reference in their settings to which they can relate so far as their home life and family backgrounds are concerned. Yet Souto-Manning and Hermann-Wilmarth (2008: 266) state that 'the field of early childhood continues to embrace a culture and curriculum that excludes gay issues'. Lesbian and gay parents with young children can feel somewhat ignored, but so too can lesbian, gay, bisexual and transgender (LGBT) practitioners. When it comes to sexuality there is often an 'assumed absence of gay and lesbian families in settings; or the assumed absence of significant gay or lesbian adults in children's lives' (Robinson, 2002: 416).

The literature on sexualities in relation to the early years is sparse. It is argued (Surtees, 2008) that heteronormativity (the view that heterosexuality is the norm and so homosexuality is therefore *ab*normal [Robinson, 2005: 181]) in early childhood education 'fuels and compounds resistance towards, and silencing of, sexuality in the sector' (2005: 19). Robinson and Jones-Diaz (2006: 166) argue that 'gay and lesbian equity issues are relevant to all children and their families regardless of their sexual orientations' and suggest that:

> heteronormativity in early childhood education is often rendered invisible through the hegemonic discourses that constitute understandings of childhood

---

[7] *Oxford English Dictionary*

and sexuality. The presumption that children are asexual, 'too young' and 'too innocent' to understand sexuality is contradicted by the fact that the construction of heterosexuality and heterosexual desire is an integral part of children's everyday practices. (ibid.: 141)

In a study to explore issues surrounding homosexuality in early childhood education, Lloyd (2009), considering the present gap in the available literature and research relating to this topic, asked: 'Why is homosexuality missing from the curriculum and excluded from the classroom or nursery?' She compared her experiences in the twenty-first century with those of an early years educator teaching over the past 20 years. Lloyd (2009: 27) argues:

> During the past 20 years there has been little progress or development in this area and society continues to believe that the issue of homosexuality is of no relevance to young children and that it does not belong in early childhood education. This fails to recognise or acknowledge the needs and experiences of children of same-sex parents or lesbian, gay, bi-sexual, transgender (LGBT) educators working in settings.

She refers back to the damage done by Section 28 of the Local Government Act 1988 which prohibited local authorities in England and Wales from 'promoting' homosexuality and labelled gay family relationships as 'pretend'. It was 2003 before that legislation was repealed and since then several pieces of important legislation have been implemented in an attempt to improve the rights of LGBT people; and yet homophobia and heteronormativity continue to exist; often unchallenged.

Lloyd (2009) using a combination of life-history research and auto-ethnography explored a personal history of two people – one with considerable experience of work and research as an academic in the field of early childhood education who openly identifies as a lesbian. This study showed that there remains:

- a significant lack of progress regarding the acceptance and acknowledgement of the issue in relation to early childhood education;
- bifurcation/dual identity of gay and lesbian staff working in early childhood education (professional role versus personal identity);
- guilt and regret experienced by gay and lesbian staff who have not felt able to 'come out' or challenge heteronormativity.

Kubiak (2009) explored the ways in which issues of sexual orientation are confronted and explored by national inspectors of early years settings

(Ofsted). It contributes to the understanding of how the concept of heteronormativity (viewing heterosexuality as 'the norm') affects the work of Ofsted inspectors. The study asked three key questions:

1. Do Ofsted inspections consider how early years educators deal with issues of sexual orientation?
2. Do Ofsted inspection reports include details of how early years educators respond to questions and matters relating to sexual orientation?
3. How important do Ofsted inspectors feel it is for children and early years educator staff to have books, equipment, posters and discussions about issues related to sexual orientation?

A questionnaire survey of approximately 100 Ofsted early years inspectors was used to:

- identify sources of information, or lack of it, for inspectors on sexual orientation, and to develop an understanding of the role that heteronormativity may play in decisions to include or exclude sexual orientation when looking at equality and diversity;
- consider what importance sexual orientation has for inspectors;
- offer recommendations to Ofsted on how to make early years inspections more inclusive.

Kubiak found that the (often heteronormative) media has a strong influence on the work of inspectors as to how they view and report on sexual orientation in early years settings. There was evidence of confusion between sex education and education in relation to sexual orientation. There was a discrepancy between the importance that inspectors placed on sexual orientation for adults and children. Inspectors lacked training and confidence in looking at issues of sexual orientation in early years settings, as opposed to other areas of diversity, and the issue of sexual orientation is still a taboo subject in some early years settings. Kubiak (2009) recommended the need to provide:

- specific training on sexual orientation as for other areas of equality and diversity;
- equality and diversity training in relation to early years settings to include sexual orientation;

- clarification of the differences between sex education and sexual orientation education;
- opportunities for inspectors to develop their knowledge and skills to challenge heteronormative practices in early years settings.

The literature indicates that there remains some ignorance and discrimination around families (and professionals) who are outside the heterosexual 'norm' and further studies and innovative practices are needed in order to recognise sexuality in the arena of early childhood education and prompt further discussion and debate.

REFERENCES AND INDICATIVE FURTHER READING

Atkinson, E. and DePalma, R. (2009) 'Un-believing the matrix: queering consensual heteronormativity', *Gender and Education*, 21(1): 17–29.

Blaise, M. (2005) *Playing It Straight. Uncovering Gender Discourses in the Early Childhood Classroom*. New York: Routledge.

Department of Health (DoH) (2007) *Reducing Health Inequalities for Lesbian, Gay, Bisexual and Transexual People*. London: DoH.

Epstein, D., O'Flynn, S. and Telford, D. (2003) *Silenced Sexualities in Schools and Universities*. Stoke-in-Trent: Trentham Books.

Fox, R.K. (2007) 'One of the hidden diversities in schools – families with parents who are lesbian or gay', *Childhood Education*, 83(5): 277–81.

Kubiak, M. (2009) 'Mr and Mr Forgotten and Ms and Ms Minority: an investigation of heteronormative inspection practices in Ofsted', unpublished MA dissertation, University of Sheffield.

Lively, V. and Lively, E. (1991) *Sexual Development of Young Children*. New York: Delmar.

Lloyd, J. (2009) 'Off the straight and narrow: to what extent do heterosexist discourses exist and operate to silence homosexuality in early childhood education?', unpublished MA dissertation, University of Sheffield.

Robinson, K. and Jones Diaz, C. (2006) *Diversity and Difference in Early Childhood Education: Issues of Theory and Practice*. London: Open University Press.

Robinson, K.H. (2002) 'Making the invisible visible: gay and lesbian issues in early childhood education', *Contemporary issues in Early Childhood*, 3(3): 415–34.

Robinson, K.H. (2005) '"Queerying" gender: heteronormativity in early childhood education', *Australian Journal of Early Childhood*', 30(2): 19–28.

Souto-Manning. M. and Hermann-Wilmarth, J. (2008) 'Teacher enquiries into gay and lesbian families in early childhood classrooms', *Journal of Early Childhood Research*, 6: 263–80.

Surtees, N. (2008) 'Teachers following children? Heteronormative responses within a discourse of child-centredness and the emergent curriculum', *Early Childhood Education*, 33(3): 10–17.

special educational
needs

> **Special Educational Needs (SEN) is the term applied to children who are identified as having learning difficulties and who may require additional support or provision to ensure they reach their potential.**

The term 'Special Educational Needs' is often used to describe many different physical and learning needs and combinations of needs which have an impact on the form and content of educational provision which is most appropriate for the child. Now widely used, the term came into being in 1978, when the Warnock Report from the Commission on Special Education (DES, 1978) concluded that children should not be identified according to 'handicap' and sent to schools which specialised in dealing with that particular 'category' of difficulty, but rather that *educational* difficulties should be identified and provided for accordingly. The term 'Special Educational Needs' thus became key in UK education legislation and has been familiar to teachers, other practitioners, parents and policy-makers since that time. Statements of Special Educational Need were compiled to detail the particular needs of children with identified difficulties and an Individual Education Plan was developed for each child to detail how their needs would be met in practical terms.

Herbert (1998) suggested that it is difficult to define Special Educational Needs in the context of the early years, largely because children with SEN are not a single identifiable group, but individuals with specific and idiosyncratic 'needs'. Children under five vary widely in their growth and development, and the years before school are often years of rapid growth and change. Needs change as do the children who are identified as having SEN. Herbert (1998: 94) notes, the 'story' of a child's Special Educational Needs can often be complex and can involve many agencies and processes including:

- early identification;
- medical diagnosis;
- prediction of need;

- role of the professionals;
- interagency collaboration;
- partnership with parents and carers;
- support and training of staff;
- the nature of assessment;
- differing forms of provision.

In recent years, in the UK, there has been massive expansion of provision for children under five and, in many cases, provision for children with learning difficulties has often been a matter of priority. However, this has not always been the case. Wall (2003) traces the development of pre-school provision in the UK from the late 1800s to the present day, and discusses the motivation of some pioneers to provide for young children with 'special needs' which in many cases were attributable to poverty and war. For example, the McMillan sisters in the early 1900s, developed nursery schools for the children of the poor and succeeded in developing provision which addressed children's health issues which inhibited their growth and development.

The development of provision across the UK during the 1990s and the drive to provide for all young children where there is specific need and all three and four year olds whose parents wish them to attend some form of provision, has highlighted the need to identify and support children whose needs are particular or who fall into what is termed Special Educational Needs. Special Educational Needs has become an issue for the majority of settings and is a concern of all practitioners – to varying degrees – from time to time. Roffey (2001) highlights the importance of collaboration, communication and coordination between agencies and between providers, practitioners and families. Special Educational Needs is no longer an issue for Special Schools alone, but it is likely that most early years settings will provide for some children who are identified as having Special Educational Needs.

In policy terms the Early Years Foundation Stage in early 2010 was clear about the expectations of practitioners in providing for young children identified as having SEN or who are disabled:

'Inclusive practice' is one of the commitments to the EYFS principle of 'A unique child'. The explanation of the commitment includes information about children's entitlements – their right be treated fairly regardless of race, religion or abilities. There is information about involving parents in early support and knowing when and how to call for specialist help.

Equality and diversity

- All children have a need to develop, which is helped by exploring and discovering the people and things around them.
- Some children's development may be at risk, for example: children who are disabled and those with Special Educational Needs.
- All children are entitled to enjoy a full life in conditions which will help them take part in society and develop as an individual, with their own cultural and spiritual beliefs.

Early support

- It is important to identify the need for additional support as early as possible. Without it children will not get the help they need at the right time, in the way that is right for them.
- Early support for children includes listening to families and taking part in a sensitive two-way exchange of information.
- For children with the most severe and complex additional support needs you need to plan jointly with everyone who is in contact with the child. This will coordinate support and promote learning as effectively as possible. Knowing when and how to call in specialist help is one important element of inclusive practice. (www.nationalstrategies.stand-ards.dcsf.gov.uk/node/84031)

Early education settings have, for many years, given priority to children with learning difficulties or to those identified as having SEN, and Nutbrown (1998) has long argued that early education – at its best – is *inclusive education* because of the emphasis, in practice, of identifying and meeting the individual learning needs of all young children. It is often the experience of those who work in early years settings that young children are included as a first option. Many such settings would argue that supporting children with learning difficulties is as much about an *attitudinal* response as it is about *practical* responses.

Research has begun to focus on telling the stories of children within the SEN category, and of how they fare in Special and mainstream schools (Berry, 2002; Pereera, 2000; Wise and Glass, 2000), but more such accounts are needed in order to help practitioners and policy-makers learn more of the experiences of parents, children and practitioners so involved.

Studies are also needed of the relationship between addressing learning difficulties, meeting Special Educational Needs, inclusive education and how learning difficulties are variously 'constructed' by parents, policy-makers and practitioners. There are often diverse views on what 'Special Educational Needs' are, and on how they should be met. Many such views are inferred from particular sets of circumstances and, Clough (2000: 6) argues, give rise to the following questions which could well form part of a research agenda:

- Where do the various 'constructions' of difficulty come from?
- How are they evidenced?
- How are they communicated?
- How are they challenged? How do they change?
- Who changes constructions of educational need, of difference and of difficulty?

LEARNING DIFFICULTIES, SPECIAL EDUCATIONAL NEEDS AND 'SPECIAL RIGHTS' IN ITALY

In 1971, Italy was one of the first countries in Europe to legislate for the integration of children with learning difficulties into mainstream schooling. In 1997 the law stated that: 'All children with handicaps, regardless of the nature and seriousness of their handicaps, are to be integrated in normal mainstream school classes' (Menegoi-Buzzi, 1999: 18). In the Reggio Emilia pre-schools of Northern Italy, children with learning difficulties are regarded as having *special rights* (rather than special needs) and Phillips (2001) argues that the Reggio *pedagogy of listening* gives 'voice' to all young children in Reggio pre-schools.

COMMUNICATING WITH HANNAH

For practitioners, teaching young children with learning difficulties necessitates knowing the child, not generalising from abstract information about 'conditions'. Hannah had Down's syndrome, she was included in the local infant school, and her class teachers in Years 1 and 2 (Tricia Robinson and Sue Small) wrote:

> Our main concern was how we were going to communicate with Hannah. The training we had in Maketon as a whole school was invaluable. What we didn't realise at the time, not knowing Hannah, was how helpful she was going to be. She helped us teach her by being so receptive and yet so patient when we failed to understand her ... Teaching Hannah was so rewarding. (Wise and Glass, 2000: 67)

REFERENCES AND INDICATIVE FURTHER READING

Berry, T. (2002) 'Does inclusion work? Simon's story', in C. Nutbrown (ed.), *Research Studies in Early Childhood Education*. Stoke-on Trent: Trentham.

Clough, P. and Corbett, J. (2000) *Theories of Inclusive Education*. London: PCP/Sage.

Clough, P. (2000) 'Routes to inclusion', in P. Clough and J. Corbett, *Theories of Inclusive Education*. London: Pcp/Sage.

Clough, P. and Garner, P. (2003) 'Special educational needs and inclusive education: origins and current issues', in S. Bartlett and D. Burton (eds), *Education Studies: Essential Issues*, London: Sage.

Clough, P. and. Nutbrown, C. (2004) 'Special educational needs and inclusive early education: multiple perspectives from UK educators', *Journal of Early Childhood Research*, 2(2):191–211.

DES (1978) *The Warnock Report*. London: HMSO.

DfES (2001) *Code of Practice on the Identification and Assessment of Children with Special Educational Needs*. London: HMSO.

Herbert, E. (1998) 'Included from the start? Managing early years settings for all', in P. Clough *Managing Inclusive Education: From Policy to Experience*. London: Paul Chapman Publishing.

Menegoi-Buzzi, I. (1999) 'A critical view of inclusion in Italy', in M. Chaltin, I. Menegoi-Buzzi, S. Phillips and N. Sylvestre (eds), *Integrating Children with Special Educational Needs (Handicapped) in Ordinary Schools: Case Studies in Europe*. Milan: IRRSAE, Lombardia.

Nutbrown, C. (1998) 'Managing to include? Rights, responsibilities and respect all', in P. Clough (ed.), *Managing Inclusive Education: From Policy to Experience*. London: Paul Chapman Publishing.

Nutbrown, C. and Clough, P. (2004) 'Inclusion in the early years: conversations with European educators', *European Journal of Special Needs Education*, 19(3): 311–39.

Pereera, S. (2000) 'Living with special educational needs: mothers' perspectives', in P. Clough and C. Nutbrown (eds), *Voices of Arabia: Essays in Educational Research*. Sheffield: University of Sheffield, School of Education.

Phillips, S. (2001) 'Special needs or special rights?', in L. Abbott and C. Nutbrown (eds), *Experiencing Reggio Emilia: Implications for Preschool Provision*. Buckingham: Open University Press.

Qualifications and Curriculum Authority/Department for Education and Skills (2000) *Curriculum Guidance for the Foundation Stage*. London: QCA/DES.

Roffey, S. (2001) *Special Needs in the Early Years: Collaboration, Communication and Co-ordination*. London: David Fulton.

Wall, K. (2003) *Special Needs and Early Years: A Practitioner's Guide*. London: Paul Chapman Publishing.

Wise, L. and Glass, C. (2000) *Working with Hannah: A Special Girl in a Mainstream School*. London: RoutledgeFalmer.

key concepts in early childhood education and care

146

> *Steiner-Waldorf kindergartens are early childhood settings which follow pedagogical practices based on the anthroposophical work of Rudolf Steiner.*

Rudolf Steiner conceived of education as an art – creative, progressive, social and individual. Teaching is essentially a vocation, a challenging yet fulfilling task, and teachers, in common with their pupils, remain learners. Not limited to schooling, teaching and learning mean taking one's place in the world, working with enthusiasm, acting with consideration, involving oneself responsibly.[8] Now an international movement, Steiner-Waldorf kindergartens are found in many countries, with over 40 in the UK.

Steiner-Waldorf kindergartens are built on the work of Rudolf Steiner and Emil Molt (managing director of the Waldorf Astoria cigarette factory). The title Steiner-Waldorf recognises the collaborative work of the two men. The first Steiner-Waldorf school opened in 1919 in Stuttgart with funding from the Waldorf Astoria company. The first kindergarten opened in 1926, the year after Steiner died. Emil Molt wrote: 'I felt the tragedy of the working class: to be held back by lack of money from sharing the education of the rich middle class. I also had a sense of what it would mean for social progress if we could support a new educational endeavour within our factory ...' (Molt, 1991: 3)

The first school thrived, educating over 1,000 pupils and stimulating the opening of new schools in Germany, Switzerland, England, the Netherlands and the US. Nazi attempts to interfere with the curriculum and the pressures of the Second World War forced the closure of the school in 1939 and it reopened in 1946 and remains on the same site today.

Rudolf Steiner (1861–1925) was Austrian, a scientist and a philosopher who founded *anthroposophy* meaning – in Greek – 'wisdom of man'. Anthroposophy is a way of looking at one's whole life in connection with the spirit. For many Steiner-educated pupils and Steiner teachers and parents of children in Steiner schools, anthroposophy is a way of life, not

---

[8]Steiner education: www.steinerwaldorf.org.uk/teaching

just a basis for a system of education. Of Steiner's early life, Oldfield (2001: 169) writes:

> He helped with farm work, roamed in the forest, and responded to the peace and beauty of the natural environment. On the other hand he was exposed to technology, industry and science through is father's railway work. These two worlds – nature and science – were to remain lifelong interests ... He was aware from an early age that there was a vast range of experience beyond physical, material reality. The visible, represented by the world of science and matter, and the invisible spiritual world, were to become as much a source of inspiration for his later initiatives as was his interest in both the inner and outer experiences, and the wholeness of the developing human being.

In his later life Steiner was greatly concerned with social issues which were the foundation of the Steiner-Walford school movement which, more than 80 years after his death, is still active internationally and offers a comprehensive, socially inclusive co-educational alternative to state education systems in many countries.

The first Waldorf kindergarten was opened in 1926, developed and run under the direction of Elizabeth von Grunelius, a teacher who had worked closely with Steiner in defining what kindergarten education in a Steiner school should look like. The Waldorf plan for early childhood education was published as 'Educating the young child' (Grunelius, 1974) in England in 1955 and set out the underpinning structures of Steiner-Waldorf Kindergarten provision which were built upon *imitation* and *example* and included three key aspects:

- Kindergartens should become places where children are protected from the harmful influences of 'our highly intellectual age'.
- Waldorf education can find roots anywhere as it rests upon an understanding of 'what is universally and fundamentally human'.
- The education rests on this understanding only, and therefore allows space for 'the ever fresh initiative of individual teachers (Oldfield, 2001: 166).

Elizabeth von Grunelius died in 1989 aged 94, having supported – in different ways – the international development of some 1,500 early childhood centres in some 30 countries.

Key questions for research in terms of mainstream education centre around what practitioners in other forms of provision can learn from

Steiner pedagogy. The central image of the child as in need of nurture and protection and an emphasis on the physical, of movement and of doing are interesting points of reference for comparative studies. One factor in relation to the funding of children attending Steiner kindergartens has been the place of technology in the setting. Traditionally, the Steiner early years curriculum has no place for computer technology and this has been an issue in relation to funding in the Early Years Foundation Stage in England.

In terms of 'opening up' knowledge of Steiner-Waldorf kindergarten practice to wider understanding, there is a need for case studies of children playing in such early years settings and for accessible reports of practice and discussion of pedagogy in multi-system fora.

Some of the important ideals in Steiner-Waldorf kindergartens, such as attachment, protection and nurture, challenge mainstream thinking and current government policy. However, the importance of creating places where children can play freely and the very different role of the adult – as model – offer areas for further thoughts and research.

It is not uncommon to find male teachers working in Steiner-Waldorf kindergartens, the proportion of men in Steiner early years settings being far higher than that of many mainstream settings. Research could ask the question as to how Steiner settings successfully recruit and retain male practitioners whereas the mainstream continues to struggle to attract men to the profession.

Steiner-Waldorf kindergartens are immediately recognisable for their homely characteristics. Furniture is often wooden, and the equipment available for the children is made of natural materials. Plastic toys are not a feature in Steiner kindergartens.

THE THREE LITTLE KITTENS

A large woollen blanket was draped over the wooden kitchen table. Muffled sounds could be heard from under the table, and eventually mewing, and scratching sounds emerged. A small girl peeped out 'meow? Meow? MEEEOOWW?' Two other heads appeared alongside her, making similar kitten-like noises. The teacher turned to the kindergarten assistant. 'Do you think the kittens need some milk?' he asked her. She nodded. The teacher took a pottery bowl from the kitchen shelf and placed it under the table. 'There, kittens – some fresh milk for you.' Meeowing, scratching, playing and curling up to sleep continued for some time, the kittens cosy under their table in their kitten home.

THE TRAIN

Six children were on the train to the seaside. They had arranged eight wooden chairs one behind the other in a row. Each had a seat and the driver was making engine noises as they continued their journey – soon all the passengers were also contributing to the roar of the engine and 'steering'. Children got on and off as the train stopped frequently and the driver announced names of places he knew. Then finally – 'Exeter – get off here everybody – this is the end of the train.' Passengers alighted from the train as instructed and after some rearrangement a new train – with two new drivers – left the station for 'Scotland'.

The kindergarten teacher glanced at the children from time to time while preparing the ingredients and equipment to make bread – the train and its passengers continued their journey without adult interference.

Lynn Oldfield (2001) in *Free to Learn* provides a clear discussion of Steiner-Waldorf pedagogy and several examples illustrate aspects of this work. Drummond and Jenkinson (2009) report on approaches to observation and assessment in Steiner kindergartens.

REFERENCES AND INDICATIVE FURTHER READING

Aeppli, W. (1986) *Rudolf Steiner Education and the Developing Child*. Hudson, NY: Anthroposophic Press.

Drummond, M.J. and Jenkinson, S. (2009) *Meeting the Child: Approaches to Observation and Assessment in Steiner Kindergartens*. A report from the Faculty of Education, University of Plymouth and the Steiner-Waldorf Early Years Research Group.

Grenelius, E. von (1974) *Early Childhood Education and the Waldorf School Plan*. Hudson, NY: Anthroposophic Press Monographs.

Lissau, R. (1987) *Rudolf Steiner: Life, Work, Inner Path and Social Initiatives*. Stroud: Hawthorn Press.

Mayer, R. (1987) *The Wisdom of Fairy Tales*. Edinburgh: Floris Books.

Molt, E. (1991) *Emil Molt and the Beginnings of the Waldorf School Movement*. Edinburgh: Floris Books.

Oldfield, L. (2001) *Free to Learn: Introducing Steiner-Waldorf Early Childhood Education*. Stroud: Hawthorn Press.

Steiner, R. (1947) *The Study of Man*. London: Anthroposophic Press.

Steiner, R. (1980) *Rudolf Steiner: An Autobiography*. Blauvelt, NY: Steinerbooks.

Steiner, R. (1995) *The Kingdom of Childhood: Introductory Talks on Waldorf Education*. Seven lectures and answers to questions given in Torquay 12–20 August 1924, translated by Rudolf Steiner Press. Hudson, NY: Anthroposophic Press.

Steiner, R. (1996) *The Foundations of Human Experience*. Hudson, NY: Anthroposophic Press. (Originally published as *The Study of Man*, 1947.)

Sure Start was a key UK government programme which began in 1999 and lasted about a decade. The stated aim was to achieve better outcomes for children, parents and communities by:

- *increasing the availability of childcare for all children;*
- *improving health and emotional development for young children;*
- *supporting parents as parents and in their aspirations towards employment.*
- *Sure Start was a major initiative which has paved the way for the development of subsequent projects and community-based multi-agency provision.*

The Sure Start programme began in the UK in 1999, working with a range of agencies in health, employment and education to achieve its comprehensive aims to provide children with a Sure Start and make them ready to 'flourish'. Working within local communities to develop local projects, the key Sure Start aims were achieved by:

- helping services develop in disadvantaged areas alongside provision of financial help for parents to afford childcare;
- rolling out the principles driving the Sure Start approach to all services for children and parents.
- With some variation Sure Start operated in England, Northern Ireland, Scotland and Wales. Investment in Sure Start by 2005–06 amounted to £1.5 billion.

Key elements of the Sure Start programme were:

- *Early education for all*: free part-time early education for three and four year olds in the Foundation Stage.
- *Increased quality and quantity of childcare*: start-up grants for childminders, nurseries and after school care, inspected by the Office for Standards in Education (Ofsted); help for working parents with their childcare costs; local Children's Information Services and a

national information service for parents; information for parents and employment advice linked to information on childcare.

- *Local programmes*: Children's Centres (with links with Sure Start, Neighbourhood Nurseries and Early Excellence Centres) in the most disadvantaged areas – to offer families early education, childcare and health and family support with advice on employment opportunities.

SURE START PRINCIPLES

Sure Start supported families from pregnancy until children were 14 years old (16 if they were disabled). The following seven principles underpinned Sure Start work:

1. *Working with parents and children.* Every family should get access to a range of services that will deliver better outcomes for both children and parents, meeting their needs and stretching their aspirations.
2. *Services for everyone.* But not the same services for everyone. Families have distinctly different needs, both between different families, in different locations and across time in the same family. Services should recognise and respond to these varying needs.
3. *Flexible at point of delivery.* All services should be designed to encourage access. For example, opening hours, location, transport issues, and care for other children in the family need to be considered. Where possible we must enable families to get the health and family support services they need through a single point of contact.
4. *Starting very early.* Services for young children and parents should start at the first antenatal visit. This means not only advice on health in pregnancy, but preparation for parenthood, decisions about returning to work (or indeed, starting work) after the birth, advice on childcare options and on support services available.
5. *Respectful and transparent.* Services should be customer-driven, whether or not the service is free.
6. *Community-driven and professionally coordinated.* All professionals with an interest in children and families should be sharing expertise and listening to local people on service priorities. This should be done through consultation and by day-to-day listening to parents.
7. *Outcome-driven.* All services for children and parents need to have as their purpose better outcomes for children. The government needs

to acknowledge this by reducing bureaucracy and simplifying funding to ensure a joined-up approach with partners (Sure Start Introduction SSULeaflet, 1 December 2003).

Much Sure Start oriented research has been in the form of evaluation of programmes, and there is a wealth of reports available from the National Evaluation of Sure Start which is available online. Hannon (1999) suggested that there were four areas in which educational research can contribute to Sure Start research:

- *lessons from the past* – drawing on evidence of effective pre-school programmes;
- *relevant research findings* – about for, example, the effects of poverty on early educational attainment;
- *research into new programmes* – such as those involving parents in early literacy development;
- *evaluation methods* – allocating resources for local projects to evaluate their own work through systematic, self-critical and clearly reported evaluation which becomes a means of sharing Sure Start work.

Hannon (1999) identified the following questions to ask about Sure Start programmes:

- Are programmes relevant?
- How well is the programme documented?
- For what communities is it designed?
- For what age is it designed?
- Has it been adequately evaluated?
- Is it shown to be valued by families?
- Do claims go beyond evidence?
- Will potential benefits justify resources?
- What are the staff development implications?
- How can community assess its potential?

Hannon further suggests that local evaluations of Sure Start should consider how they articulate with the national evaluation, their use of external or practitioner research, whether formative or summative, the resources needed and the need for outside support of consultation. Finally, Hannon lists ten points that local evaluations of Sure Start work should cover:

1. Community profile.
2. Description of services/implementation.
3. Take-up, participation and drop-out.
4. Judgements of quality of services.
5. Views of staff.
6. Views of community.
7. Outcomes for children.
8. Outcomes for adults.
9. Key lessons learned.
10. Reporting – sharing – dissemination (Hannon, 1999: 6).

Weinberger et al. (2005) reported on the collaboration between one Sure Start programme and its local university over a five-year period to develop and evaluate the initiative. They describe the range of services in health, education and social welfare provided through the Sure Start programme and examine implications for inter-agency work, and lessons learned, concluding that:

> Sure Start programmes were wide ranging and included a myriad of activities including: Family support; work with teenage mothers; breastfeeding support; home safety; smoking cessation; play and learning programmes; language development screening; media literacy projects; reading projects; community involvement; the beginnings of many being identified through community surveys (Weinberger et al., 2005).

The following examples give an indication of the kinds of programmes that were developed through Sure Start.

BREASTFEEDING IN RAVENSDALE

Mothers from the Ravensdale area were surveyed to assess the impact of the Sure Start Breastfeeding Incentive scheme on their own experiences of breastfeeding their babies. The 26 participants in the survey reported that they valued the midwife support offered and the peer support available from other Sure Start mothers. Twenty-three per cent attributed their continued breastfeeding to the programme (Sharp, 2003).

READY FOR SCHOOL

In Exeter, a joint a nursery and a first school developed a Ready for School project to find ways of overcoming the social isolation of many children in the area. Initially the project had three elements: a nurture group, a language enrichment programme and additional support for children's play, language and development. The programme, according to several measures, appeared to make a difference to children's use of language and communication, many making better than expected progress. Outcomes are earlier identification of children with speech and language difficulties, and positive involvement of parents around their children's learning and development (Randell et al., 2004).

REFERENCES AND INDICATIVE FURTHER READING

Hannon. P. (1999) 'What can educational research offer Sure Start?', briefing note commissioned by the NHS Executive (Trent Region) for a symposium held in Derby, 29 March.

Randell, S., Payne-Cook, E. and Marlow, P. (2004) *Ready for School: The Nursery Project: A Joint Initiative between Willowbrook School, Sure Start Exeter and Whipton First School*. National Evaluation of Sure Start. Available at: www.surestart.gov.UK

Sharp, A. (2003) *Sure Start Ravensdale Breastfeeding Survey*. November 2003. National Evaulation of Sure Start. Available at: www.surestart.gov.UK

Sure Start website: www.surestart.gov.uk

Weinberger, J., Pickstone, C. and Hannon, P. (eds) (2005) *Learning from Sure Start: Working with Young Children and their Families*. Buckingham: Open University Press.

sure start

> Te Whāriki *is the New Zealand Ministry of Education's early childhood curriculum policy statement* (He Whāriki Mātauranga mō ngā Mokopuna o Aotearoa). Te Whāriki *is a framework for providing for* tamariki/*children's early learning and development within a sociocultural context. It emphasises the learning partnership between* kaiako/*teachers, parents,* whānau/*families.* Kaiako/*teachers weave a holistic curriculum in response to* tamariki/*children's learning and development in the early childhood setting and the wider context of the child's world.*[9]

Te Whāriki is a bilingual document which sets out the curriculum policy and framework from birth to five in New Zealand. It has been widely acclaimed in many other countries and, similar to the inspirational work of Reggio Emilia, has inspired an interest in practices and policies in early childhood which see children as central to their community and see learning as a shared experience. For this reason, many early childhood educators have an interest in the *Te Whāriki* framework and the principles which underpin it. The *Te Whāriki* document opens with a Maori poem followed by these words:

> Early childhood is '... a period of momentous significance for all people growing up in [our] culture ... By the time this period is over, children will have formed conceptions of themselves as social beings, as thinkers, and as language users, and they will have reached certain important decisions about their own abilities and their own worth.' (Donaldson et al., 1983, in Ministry of Education New Zealand, 1996: 1)

The introduction states:

> This statement is an exciting new development for education in New Zealand. It is the first national curriculum statement for the early childhood sector. This curriculum statement provides the basis for consistent high quality curriculum delivery in the diverse range of early childhood services in New Zealand. Over the past century, early childhood care and

---

[9]Education Review Office: www.ero.govt.nz/publications/Te Whariki

education services in New Zealand have been established to meet the particular needs of children, parents, and communities, as well as those of society as a whole. Today early childhood services are jointly involved with families in the socialisation, care, and education of children. (Ministry of Education New Zealand, 1996: 4)

The underpinnings are explicitly holistic, with the stated aspirations for children: 'to grow up as competent and confident learners and communicators, healthy in mind, body, and spirit, secure in their sense of belonging and in the knowledge that they make a valued contribution to society' (ibid.: 9).

The *Te Whāriki* sets out the principles, strands and goals for the early childhood years, appropriately differentiated for babies, toddlers and young children. 'Curriculum' is defined as 'the sum total of the experiences, activities, and events, whether direct or indirect, which occur within an environment designed to foster children's learning and development (ibid.: 10).

There are four foundation *principles* for the early childhood curriculum:

1. Empowerment – *Whakamana* – the early childhood curriculum empowers the child to learn and grow.
2. Holistic development – *Kotahitanga* – the early childhood curriculum reflects the holistic way children learn and grow.
3. Family and community – *Whānau Tangata* – the wider world of family and community is an integral part of the early childhood curriculum.
4. Relationships – *Ngā Hononga* – children learn through responsive and reciprocal relationships with people, places and things (Carr and May, 2000).

Carr and May (2000) describe how the development of the New Zealand early childhood curriculum rejected a subject-based framework and favoured instead, 'strands': *well being, belonging, contributing, communicating* and *exploring*. The strands and goals arise from the principles and are woven around these principles in patterns that reflect the diversity of each early childhood education service. Together, the principles, strands, goals, and learning outcomes set the framework for the curriculum *Whāriki* (*whāriki* being the Maori word for 'mat'). The ethos behind *Te Whāriki* is that every child has a curriculum mat fitting his or her needs, culture and personality. Every one is different, but each has the same principles and strands in its warp and weft. Other strands, more individually defined can be added this making the curriculum for every child unique and appropriate.

In the UK, *Te Whāriki* stimulated research, when the Early Childhood Education Forum instigated a curriculum project *Quality in Diversity*. The project sought to bring together the views of early childhood educators in a range of settings and address the curriculum and development needs of children aged from birth to seven years (ECEF, 1998). The holistic approach to learning and the embeddedness of social and cultural concerns of the New Zealand curriculum can be recognised in the UK work, *Quality in Diversity* which was described as a 'framework to enable early childhood practitioners to think about, understand, support and extend the learning of young children from birth to the age of eight' (ECEF, 1998: 1). *Quality in Diversity* was not described as a curriculum and had no official government status, but was instead described as a 'framework' with 'foundations', 'goals' and 'children's entitlements'. Though *Quality in Diversity* did not have the impact on early childhood education that *Te Whāriki* did, the work to develop it was key in opening up discussion and development around work to promote a more holistic approach to young children's development.

Perhaps the most obvious research issue to arise from this work and the stimulus it provided in the UK is the need for more cross-cultural studies of curriculum approaches and frameworks and the importance of understanding early childhood education interculturally.

Te Whāriki is rich with examples of how the various 'goals' for children are realised in practice. The example in Figure 7 shows how Goal 4 of the 'Belonging' strand is applied to work with babies, toddlers and young children.

REFERENCES AND INDICATIVE FURTHER READING

Carr, M. and May, H. (2000) 'Te Whariki: curriculum voices', in H. Penn (ed.), *Early Childhood Services: Theory, Policy and Practice*. Buckingham: Open University Press.

Donaldson, M., Grieve, R. and Pratt, C. (1983) *Early Childhood Development and Education: Readings in Psychology*. Oxford: Basil Blackwell.

Early Childhood Education Forum (ECEF) (1998) *Quality in Diversity*. London: National Children's Bureau.

Ministry of Education New Zealand (1996) *Te Whāriki He Whāriki Mātauranga mō ngā Mokopuna o Aotearo/Early Childhood Curriculum.* Wellington: Learning Media.

Tobin, J.J., Wu, D.Y.H. and Davidson, D.H. (1989) *Preschool in Three Cultures: Japan, China and the United States.* London: Yale University Press.

Tobin, J.J., Hsueh, Y. and Karasawa, M. (2009) *Preschool in Three Cultures Revisited: China, Japan and the United States.* Chicago: Unversity of Chicago Press.

Goal 4	Children and their families experience an environment where they know the limits and boundaries of acceptable behaviour.

Examples

For Infants:

- Infants' behaviour on both their good days and their bad days is accepted without judgement, and the programme has sufficient flexibility to accommodate natural variations.
- Adults gently encourage infants to accept that the adult will also attend to and care for other children.
- Familiar, unhurried adults are always nearby.

For Toddlers:

- Adults help toddlers begin to manage their feelings appropriately.
- Adults offer only genuine choices and respect the toddlers' decisions.
- Possible causes of conflict and frustration for toddlers are minimised.
- Toddlers are given support in dealing with conflict and frustrations.
- Toddlers' intensity of feelings is understood, accepted, and dealt with, and their conflicting feelings are seen as a normal and important part of their development.
- Consistent and manageable expectations and limits are set.

For young children:

- The programme provides opportunities to discuss and negotiate fairness, and justice with adults.
- Young children have opportunities to discuss their feelings and the feelings and expectations of others.
- Strategies for managing behaviour are used not only to prevent unacceptable behaviour but also to develop ideas of fairness and justice and to introduce new social skills.
- The programme provides frequent opportunities for children to make their own decisions and be self-reliant.
- The environment and routines are planned to minimise confrontation and conflict, for instance, from crowding and queueing.

Te Whāriki

159

Figure 7   *Goal 4 of the 'Belonging' strand is applied differentially to work with babies, toddlers and young children (Ministry of Education New Zealand, 1996: 63)*

> *The Treasure Basket is a basket of objects, designed for use by babies (approx six to nine months) who can sit up comfortably but not yet crawl. The contents are intended for babies to investigate and explore using all their senses.*

The Treasure Basket has been developed by Elinor Goldschmied (Goldschmied and Jackson, 1994). Based on observations in many cultures, of how young babies first learn about the world, this early stage of providing for babies' learning offers a means of ensuring that babies experience variety and quality. The underpinning philosophy is described thus:

> A baby's first toy is the body of her caring adult. A baby grasps her parent's fingers, handles her mother's breast, entwining her fingers in her mother's hair or her father's beard, grabs at earrings, necklaces or spectacles … Awareness of her own body grows as a baby crams her small fist into her mouth and, lying on her back, identifies her feet and toes … From an early age, a baby will grasp an offered rattle … Eye, hand and mouth co-ordination marks a big step forward, but like all skills, if it is to develop, the baby needs opportunities to practise.
>
> As a baby's waking time extends and she begins to sit upright, first propped up by cushions or in a relaxing chair, then independently, a whole new horizon opens up. It may be that she can now see the underneath of a table, our shoes and ankles, the moving hem of a trouser leg, in addition to the other interesting items in the room. She has a kind of worm's eye view of the world, but none the less intriguing for that. (Goldschmied and Jackson, 1994: 86–7)

It was in response to the need for babies at this stage to be provided with interesting experiences which provided stimulus for all the senses that the Treasure Basket was devised. The Treasure Basket (dimensions of which should be 36 cm in diameter and 10–15 cm high, flat bottomed with no handle and strong enough for an infant to lean on without tipping up) is filled to the brim with objects to allow baby plenty of scope to sort through and to select what appeals to him or her. A baby using a Treasure Basket must be seated comfortably (with a supporting cushion if necessary), sideways on to the basket with the rim near enough for an elbow to rest upon it, and in a position which makes it easy for him or her to see and reach objects in the basket. If the baby cannot yet move for themselves, the watching adult will need to pay careful attention to any signs that the baby needs help to shift position or stop play with the basket. There are two important elements about the practice of using Treasure Baskets: the objects it contains and the role of the adult.

The objects in the Treasure Basket must be washable and made from natural materials (not plastic) and should be augmented and changed regularly to maintain interest. Suggested objects include: large pebbles, shells, big feathers, corks, a lemon, an apple, small baskets, shaving brush, small wooden boxes, wooden curtain ring, wooden egg cup, metal spoon, small tin, length of chain, bunch of keys, leather purse, small herb bag, tinfoil, cardboard tube. In all (Goldschmied and Jackson, 1994) recommend around 100 objects which are either natural or made from natural materials – wood, raffia, metal, leather, rubber, fur, paper.

The attentive adult – usually the baby's Key Person – has a crucial but largely silent role. She or he should sit nearby, preferably on a low, comfortable chair so that she or he can respond and affirm the child at play. The role of the adult is crucial in supporting and affirming the child's desire to concentrate and explore. Almost every child will approach this differently and so the practitioner should be wholly focused on the baby (or babies) but should not select items for the baby, allowing him or her to choose for themselves.

Although Treasure Baskets are widely used in many settings, the impact of their use on babies' learning and development is not widely understood and there are limited case studies or extended observations of the use of treasure baskets. Work with babies would benefit from understanding more of (a) how babies use treasure baskets both in home and group settings and (b) how the adults involved in supporting babies' explorations of objects in a treasure basket see their role.

With the development of the *Birth to Three Matters* Framework (Abbott and Langston, 2005; DfES, 2002) research now needs to focus on the incorporation of established practices into the policy framework for work with babies and young children under three in order to ensure a balanced living and learning experience. Additionally, work with parents, to ensure their understanding of the principles behind the Treasure Basket is crucial. Misunderstandings and worries about safety need to be addressed through a participative approach to working in partnership with parents and ensuring that family and cultural concerns and wishes are respected.

MATTHEW'S TREASURE BASKET

Christmas had seen the arrival of Matthew's Treasure Basket. At six months old he was just the right age to begin his exploration of the natural materials offered to him. At the time of the observation, Matthew, just turned nine months old, was used to handling, mouthing, sorting and selecting his favourite items from his basket.

Matthew's mother, Kate, places the Treasure Basket with its abundance of natural materials in the middle of a large cleared space in the room. She then asks Matthew gently if he would like to play with his treasure. He waves his arms and legs frantically as his eyes rest on the basket. Kate places Matthew close enough for him to reach right into the basket. He immediately reaches in with his right hand and selects a long wooden-handled spatula. 'Oohh, ahh' he says and looks directly at his mother. She smiles at him in approval. Still holding the spatula he proceeds to kneel up and lean across the basket in order to reach a long brown silk scarf. He pulls at the scarf and squeals in delight as he pulls the fabric through his fingers. 'Oohh, ahh' he repeats. He lets go of the spatula and abandons the scarf to his side, his eyes rest on a large blue stone, he picks up the large stone with his right hand and turns it over on his lap using both hands. Still using both hands he picks up the stone and begins to bite it, making a noise as his teeth grind against the hard surface. He smiles looking at his mother as he repeatedly bites the stone over and over again. He stops holds the stone up to his face and looks at it intently then puts it to his mouth once more. He then picks up the wooden spatula again and while holding it firmly in one hand, he turns the contents of the basket over with his other hand, squealing loudly with delight as he discovers the matching long-handled fork. Matthew looks at his mother and waves both items in the air smiling and rocking on his knees saying 'Oohh, ahh'. He turns away from the basket and waves the long-handled implements up and down in his hands, first one then the other, then both together. He turns back to the basket with a puzzled expression and for a few seconds, stops waving the items. He drops the fork and reaches back into the basket and randomly picks up items one at a time, looks at them and then discards them on the floor beside him. He continues this pattern for several seconds until he comes upon a long-handled brush. He picks up the brush, pauses and then waves it in his left hand, all the time continuing to hold the wooden spatula in his right hand. For several seconds he proceeds to bang the long-handled items together, smiling as the two wooden items make a sound as they come together. He then spots the wooden fork he had disposed of earlier and letting go of the brush picks up the wooden fork and bangs it together with the spatula. 'Baba, baba, da, da, da,' he says, then a little more loudly he repeats 'Baba, baba, da, da, da.' Just when it seems that he is giving signals that he has finished with the items in the basket he notices another long scarf. Letting go of both the wooden items he reaches into the basket and tugs the scarf, pulls it over his face and blows 'raspberries'. He smiles at his mother and she smiles at him. The material falls to the floor and Matthew looks up at his mother and waves his arms up and down. Kate realising that Matthew is signalling that he has finished with his Treasure Basket for today reaches down and holds her arms out to him. Matthew instantly smiles, holds his arms up to her. As she sweeps him into her arms, Matthew snuggles into his mother's neck and with his thumb in his mouth says, 'Kai, kai, kai,' a pleasurable comfort sound that Matthew vocalises when seemingly enjoying close contact with his family members.

INVOLVING PARENTS

Siobhan was seven months old and attended a day-care setting for two days a week. The Treasure Basket was established practice in the setting and practitioners had taken great care to ensure that parents knew about its use and understood the rationale behind the selection of its contents. Siobhan's father came to collect her early one day, and found his young baby sitting on the floor sucking a metal garlic crusher. He looked horrified! The practitioner signalled the father to sit on the chair next to her and together they watched his baby. His fears about the danger that the object might do to his baby receded as he witnessed the attentiveness of his daughter. The practitioners pointed silently to the baby's curled toes and the father smiled. When the session was over, the practitioner and the father talked – he said that he understood the principles behind the Treasure Basket – they had been carefully explained by his baby's Key Person when Siobhan began at the centre. He was, however, concerned that some objects were potentially dangerous and asked the centre to review the contents. Following discussion among the team it was decided to withdraw some more controversial objects from the Treasure Baskets – the staff believing that it was better slightly to reduce the contents (though still providing a large variety of objects) than create unnecessary anxiety for parents.

THE WATCHING, ATTENTIVE ADULT

Treasure Basket time is a good time to observe babies and to build a picture of what children 'can do'. Patterns of behaviour and early schemas can be observed. For example, does Robby always choose the items with a long handle? How does this relate to items he enjoys at other times of the day when the Treasure Basket is not available? How does Robby select toys generally? Does he lose interest if the long-handled items are not in the Treasure Basket? The practitioner can use his or her observations to build on Robby's interest in long-handled items and discuss this particular interest with parents to learn if there is a similar pattern or preference at home. With appropriate permission and if unobtrusive and not distracting to the baby, photographs can be taken to share with his or her parents and included in the personal profile.

REFERENCES AND INDICATIVE FURTHER READING

Abbott, L. and Langston, A. (2005) *Birth to Three Matters: Supporting the Framework for Effective Practice.* Buckingham: Open University Press.

DfES (2002) *Birth to Three Matters.* London: DfES Publications.

Goldschmied, E. (1989) *Infants at Work: The Treasure Basket Explained.* London: National Children's Bureau.

Goldschmied, E. and Jackson, S. (1994) *People Under Three: Young Children in Day Care.* London: Routledge.

Goldschmied, E. and Selleck, D. (1996) *Communication Between Babies in Their First Year.* London: National Children's Bureau.

un convention on the rights of the child

un convention on the rights of the child

UN Convention on the Rights of the Child is an international convention listing 54 Articles of rights which are designed to prevent illness and neglect; provide education; protect from abuse and exploitation and to ensure participation in decisions that affect them.

The term 'Children's Rights' has gained currency in the past 50 years, beginning with the Declaration of Rights of the Child by the General Assembly of the United Nations (UN) on 20 November 1959. Subsequently, the *United Nations Convention on the Rights of the Child* was established by the United Nations in 1989. The 1959 declaration established ten principles which laid down rights to which the UN said children should be entitled:

The right to:

1. equality, regardless of race, colour, religion, sex or nationality;
2. healthy mental and physical development;
3. a name and a nationality;
4. sufficient food, housing and medical care;
5. special care if handicapped;
6. love, understanding and care;
7. free education, play and recreation;
8. immediate aid in the event of disasters and emergencies;
9. protection from cruelty, neglect and exploitation;
10. protection from persecution and to an upbringing in the spirit of worldwide brotherhood and peace.

The language of the Declaration of 1959 is changed in the Convention of 1989, where 54 detailed Articles define the range of children's rights under four categories. The Convention states children's rights to:

1. prevention (of illness and neglect);
2. provision (of education with specific references to children who are disabled);

3. protection (from abuse and exploitation);
4. participation (in decisions which affect them).

Research into the broad range of issues covered under the theme of 'children's rights' is very wide-ranging and, internationally, focuses on issues which include such topics as corporal punishment, child poverty, children and the law , child labour and child health (including immunisation, food and the environment). Though research issues and articles are published in many journals across the range of disciplines, the *International Journal of Children's Rights* focuses on 'critical leadership and practical policy development' in the field of children's rights and is a key source of information on current projects and research. Work from a range of disciplines which seek to further children's rights internationally is reported in the journal (which focuses on children of all ages). Such areas of work include law, legal and political theory, psychology, psychiatry, educational theory, sociology, social administration and social work, health, social anthropology, economics, theology and history.

Research in the field is varied and the two examples included here are indicative of the field of study. In Sweden children's rights have been a focus of interest and concern since the UN Convention was signed in 1989. Studies have included work on young children's understanding of their rights and the development of practical materials to help children to learn about the Convention and to discuss their rights (Backstrom, 1997). Similar resources have been developed in other countries (Covell and Howe, 1999).

A Save the Children study of young children's rights (Alderson, 2000) examined children's involvement in decisions which affected them. Based in the UK, the study showed how children's contributions were often unrecognised by adults and how many adults, due largely to their desire to protect children from danger, denied children basic freedoms to play, be with their friends and play in the park. Alderson (2000) gives many examples of young children participating in decisions about their lives, such as suggesting ideas for the development of play facilities, buildings and menus, and getting involved in strategies to resolve bullying.

There are examples of practice where children's rights are a fundamental and guiding principle of curriculum and pedagogy. Such an example can be found in the infant–toddler centres and pre-schools in Reggio Emilia in Northern Italy (see 'Reggio Emilia Approach'). Central concerns are:

The rights of children: the fact that the rights of children are recognised as the rights of all children is the sign of a more accomplished humanity;

The rights of teachers: for the teachers, each and every one of them, it is a condition that enhances communication and the comparison of ideas and experiences, all of which enrich the tools of professional evaluation;

The rights of parents: participation and research are, in fact, two terms that summarise much of the overall conception of our educational theory. These two terms might also be seen as the best prerequisites for initiating and maintaining a cooperative understanding between parents and teachers, with all the value that is added to the educational prospects of the children. (Malaguzzi, 1996: 2)

A second example is found in the argument of daily practice. That is to say, that though it is governments which have signed the UN Convention on the Rights of the Child, thus declaring their commitment to working within their countries to realise and protect children's rights as enshrined in the Convention, much of the reality of putting children's rights into practice lies in the hands of individual practitioners working in services and settings for children and their families. 'There are obligations on governments, yes, but there are responsibilities for every adult citizen too' (Nutbrown, 1996: 108).

Such arguments continue to be made, with concerns that too great a focus is still being placed on the UN Convention, on Geneva and the structure of the Committee on the Rights of the Child, and too little on development and progress at a more local level (Veernam and Levine, 2000).

REFERENCES AND INDICATIVE FURTHER READING

Alderson, P. (2000) *Young Children's Rights: Exploring Beliefs, Principles.* London: Jessica Kingsley.

Backstrom, K. (1997) 'The significance of the UN Convention on the Rights of the Child to children in preschool and school', paper given at the 22nd International Montessori Congress 'The Child and Communication', 22–27 July. Available at: www.ilu.uu.se/ilu/montessori/index/htm

Covell, K. and Howe, R.B. (1999) *Children's Rights Education Curriculum Resource.* Cape Breton, Nova Scotia: University College of Cape Breton Children's Rights Centre.

Malaguzzi, L. (1996) 'The right to environment', in T. Filippini and V. Vecchi (eds), *The Hundred Languages of Children: The Exhibit.* Reggio Emilia: Reggio Children.

Moss, P. (1989) *The United Nations Convention on the Rights of the Child: Articles and summary commentary.* New York: UNESCO/NCB.

Nutbrown, C. (ed.) (1996) *Respectful Educators – Capable Learners: Children's Rights in Early Education*. London: Paul Chapman Publishing.

United Nations (1989) *Convention on the Rights of the Child*. New York: United Nations.

Veerman, P. and Levine, H. (2000) 'Implementing children's rights on a local level: narrowing the gap between Geneva and the grassroots', *International Journal of Children's Rights*, 8: 373–84.

glossary

Atelier. In Reggio Emilia pre-schools, the studio, workshop or art room, furnished with a wide variety of resources and materials, used by all the children and adults in the pre-school.

Desirable Learning Outcomes (DLO). Age-related goals which young children should achieve on entry to school at the age of five years. The DLOs were replaced in September 2000 by Early Learning Goals.

Early Excellence Centres. Centres designated by the DfEE providing a range of integrated services for children from birth to five years and their families.

Early Learning Goals. Outcomes in six areas of learning which children should achieve by the end of the Foundation Stage: personal, social and emotional communication; language and literacy; mathematical; knowledge and understanding of the world; physical; creative. Part of the Foundation Stage in the UK in 2000, later replaced by the Early Years Foundation Stage 2008.

Early Years Childcare Inspector. A person employed by Ofsted who is responsible for regulating and inspecting day care and childminding provision.

Ofsted (Office for Standards in Education). The government agency responsible for the inspection of provision.

Practitioners. The generic term currently in use in the UK to refer to all adults who work with young children in home or group settings, regardless of job title or qualification. Not to be confused with those holding Early Years Professional Status (for which they have undergone specific training and assessment).

Reception classes. The first year of formal schooling in the UK is called the Reception class, some now refer to this as Foundation 2. Children often attend the Reception class (or Foundation 2) between the ages of four and five.

Registered person. A person deemed qualified to care for children and whose name appears on the certificate of registration. The registered person has overall responsibility for ensuring that the requirements of the national standards are met. A company, committee or other group may be the registered person.

Setting. The generic term used to refer to all forms of provision (home and group) where young children are cared for and educated, including: Children's Centres, childminding, LA nurseries, kindergartens, play-groups, independent provision, voluntary groups.

further resources

READING LIST

In addition to the specific sources listed at the end of each entry in this book, the following list gives general sources which cover a range of topics in early childhood education and care.

Abbott, L. and Moylett, H. (eds) (1997) *Working with the Under-Threes: Training and Professional Development*. Buckingham: Open University Press.

Abbott, L. and Moylett, H. (1999) *Early Education Transformed*. London: Falmer.

Abbott, L. and Pugh, G. (eds) (1998) *Training to Work in the Early Years: Developing the Climbing Frame*. Buckingham: Open University Press.

Achhpal, B., Goldman, A. and Rohner, R.P. (2007) 'A comparison of European American and Puerto Rican parents' goals and expectations about the socialization and education of pre-school children', *International Journal of Early Years Education*, 15(1): 1–13.

Alderson, P. (2008) *Young Children's Rights: Exploring Beliefs, Principles and Practice*, 2nd Edn. London: Jessica Kingsley.

Anette, S. and Tuula, V. (2008) 'Preschool–home cooperation in change', *International Journal of Early Years Education*, 16(2): 151–61.

Anning, A. (1997) *The First Years at School*, 2nd edn. Buckingham: Open University Press.

Anning, A. and Edwards, A. (1999) *Promoting Children's Learning from Birth to Five: Developing the New Early Years Professional*. Buckingham: Open University Press.

Anning, A. and Ring, K. (2004) *Making Sense of Children's Drawings*. Buckingham: Open University Press.

Aubrey, C., David, T., Godfrey, R. and Thompson, L. (2000) *Early Childhood Educational Research: Issues in Methodology and Ethics*. London: RoutledgeFalmer.

Bennett, N., Wood, L. and Rogers, S. (1997) *Teaching through Play: Teachers' Thinking and Classroom Practice*. Buckingham: Open University Press.

Blackledge, A. (2000) *Literacy, Power and Social Justice*. Stoke-on-Trent: Trentham.

Blenkin, G.M. and Kelly, A.V. (eds) (1992) *Assessment in Early Childhood Education*. London: Sage.

Blenkin, G. and Kelly, A.V. (eds) (1999) *Principles into Practice in Early Childhood Education*. London: Paul Chapman Publishing/Sage

British Educational Research Association Early Years Special Interest Group (2003) *Early Years Research: Pedagogy, Curriculum and Adult Roles, Training and Professionalism*. Nottingham: BERA.

Bundy, A.C., Luckett, T., Tranter, P.J., Naughton, G.A., Wyver, S.R., Ragen, J. and Spies, G. (2009) 'The risk is that there is "no risk": a simple, innovative intervention to increase children's activity levels', *International Journal of Early Years Education*, 17(1): 33–45.

Christensen, P. and James, A. (eds) (2000) *Research with Children: Perspectives and Practices*. London: Falmer.

Clouder, C., Jenkinson, S. and Large, M. (2000) *The Future of Childhood*. Stroud: Hawthorn Press.

Cox, T. and Sanders, S. (1994) *The Impact of the National Curriculum on the Teaching of Five Year Olds*. London: Falmer Press.

David, T. (1993) *Child Protection and Early Years Teachers Coping with Child Abuse*. Buckingham: Open University Press.

David, T. (ed.) (1998) *Researching Early Childhood Education: European Perspectives*. London: Paul Chapman Publishing/Sage.

David, T. (ed.) (1999) *Teaching Young Children*. London: Paul Chapman Publishing/ Sage.

David, T. (ed.) (1999) *Young Children Learning*. London: Paul Chapman Publishing/ Sage.

de Haan, D. and Singer, E. (2003) '"Use your words": a sociocultural approach to the teacher's role in the transition from physical to verbal strategies of resolving peer conflicts among toddlers', *Journal of Early Childhood Research*, 1(1): 95–109.

Dowty, T. (2008) 'Pixie-dust and privacy: what's happening to children's rights in England?', *Children & Society*, 22(5): 393–9.

Duffy, B. (1998) *Supporting Creativity and Imagination in the Early Years*. Buckingham: Open University Press.

Dunn, J. (2004) *Children's Friendships The Beginnings of Intimacy*. London: Blackwell.

Edwards, C., Gandini, L. and Forman, G. (eds) (1994) *The Hundred Languages of Children: The Reggio Emilia Approach to Early Childhood Education*. Norwood, NJ: Ablex.

Elfer, P (2007) 'What are nurseries for? The concept of primary task and its application in differentiating roles and tasks in nurseries', *Journal of Early Childhood Research*, 5(2): 169–88.

Fenech, M. and Sumsion, J. (2007) 'Promoting high quality early childhood education and care services: beyond risk management, performative constructions of regulation', *Journal of Early Childhood Research*, 5(3): 263–83.

Fleer, M., Hedegaard, M. and Tudge, J. (eds) (2009) *Childhood Studies and the Impact of Globalization: Policies and Practices at Global and Local Levels*. Oxford: Routledge.

Freeman, M. (2000) 'The Future of Children's Rights', *Children & Society*, 14(4): 277–93.

Gill, T. (2007) *No Fear: Growing Up in a Risk Averse Society*. London: Calouste Gulbenkian Foundation.

Graue, M.E. and Walsh, D.J. (1998) *Studying Children in Context: Theories, Methods and Ethics*. London: Sage.

Gregory, E. and Williams, A. (2000) *City Literacies: Learning to Read Across Generations and Cultures*. London: Routledge.

Greig, A. and Taylor, J. (1999) *Doing Research with Children*. London: Sage.

Hannon, P. (1995) *Literacy, Home and School: Research and Practice in Teaching Literacy with Parents*. London: Falmer Press.

Hannon, P. (2000) *Reflecting on Literacy in Education*. London: RoutledgeFalmer.

Hurst, V. and Joseph, J. (1998) *Supporting Early Learning: The Way Forward*. Buckingham: Open University Press.

Hutt, S.J., Tyler, S., Hutt, C. and Christopherson, H. (1989) *Play, Exploration and Learning: A Natural History of the Pre-school*. London: Routledge.

Jans, M. (2004) 'Children as citizens: towards a contemporary notion of child participation', *Research Centre Childhood and Society Childhood*, 11(1): 27–44.

Kenner, C. (2000) *Home Pages: Literacy Links for Bilingual Children*. Stoke-on-Trent: Trentham.

Keyser, J. (2004) *From Parents to Partners: Building a Family-Centered Early Childhood Program*. Washington, DC: NAEYC and Redleaf.

Lane, J. (2008) *Young Children and Racial Justice: Taking Action for Racial Equality–Understanding the Past, thinking About the Present, Planning for the Furture*. London: National Children's Bureau.

Lee, K. and Walsh, D.J. (2004) 'Teaching children at-risk: an American preschool teacher's folk psychology and folk pedagogy', *Journal of Early Childhood Research*, 2(3): 229–46.

Lee, L. (2009) 'Young American immigrant children's interpretations of popular culture: a case study of Korean girls' perspectives on royalty in Disney films', *Journal of Early Childhood Research*, 7(2): 200–15.

Lee, S.Y. (2006) 'A journey to a close, secure, and synchronous relationship: infant-caregiver relationship development in a childcare context', *Journal of Early Childhood Research*, 4(2):133–51.

Lewis, A. and Lindsay, G. (eds) (2000) *Researching Children's Perspectives*. Buckingham. Open University Press.

Little, H. (2006) 'Children's risk-taking behaviour: implications for early childhood policy and practice', *International Journal of Early Years Education*, 14(2): 41–54.

MacNaughton, G. and Davis, K. (2009) *"Race" and Early Childhood Education: An International Approach to Identity, Politics, and Pedagogy*. London: Palgrave Macmillan.

Marsh, J. and Hallet, E. (eds) (2008) *Desirable Literacies: Approaches to Language and Literacy in the Early Years* (2nd edn). London: Paul Chapman Publishing.

McBride, B.A., Bae, J. and Blatchford, K. (2003) 'Family–school–community partnerships in rural at-risk programs', *Journal of Early Childhood Research*, 1(1): 49–72.

Moss, P. and Pence, A. (eds) (1994) *Valuing Quality in Early Childhood Services: New Approaches to Defining Quality*. London: Paul Chapman Publishing.

Moss, P. and Penn, H. (1996) *Transforming Nursery Education*. London: Paul Chapman Publishing.

Moyles, J. (ed.) (1994) *The Excellence of Play*. Buckingham: Open University Press.

Nutbrown, C. and Clough, P. (2006) *Inclusion in the Early Years: Critical Analyses and Enabling Narratives*. London: Sage.

Nutbrown, C., Hannon, P. and Morgan, A. (2005) *Early Literacy Work with Families: Policy, Practice and Research*. London: Sage.

Paavola, L., Kemppinen, K., Kunnari, S., Kumpulainen, K., Moilanen, I. and Ebeling, H. (2006) 'Characteristics of mother–infant communicative interaction relations to the ratings of maternal sensitivity and infant co-operation', *Journal of Early Childhood Research* 4(3): 203–22.

Parton, N., Thorpe, D. and Wattam, C. (1997) *Child Protection, Risk and the Moral Order*. London: Macmillan.

Pollard, A. (1996) *The Social World of Children's Learning*. London: Cassell.

Pugh, G., De'Ath, E. and Smith, C. (1994) *Confident Parents, Confident Children: Policy and Practice in Parents' Education and Support*. London: National Children's Bureau.

Rhedding-Jones, J. (2001) 'Shifting ethnicities: "native informants" and other theories from/for early childhood education', *Contemporary Issues in Early Childhood*, 2(2): 135–56.

Robinson, C. and Stalker, K. (eds) (1999) *Growing up with Disability*. London: Jessica Kingsley.

Roose, R. and Bouverne-De Bie, M. (2007) 'Do children have rights or do their rights have to be realised? The United Nations Convention on the Rights of the Child as a frame of reference for pedagogical action' *Journal of Philosophy of Education*, 41(3): 431–43.

Rosen, R. (2010) '"We got our heads together and came up with a plan": young children's perceptions of curriculum development in one Canadian preschool', *Journal of Early Childhood Research*, 8(1): 89–108.

Ryan, S. and Grieshaber, S. (2005) 'Shifting from developmental to postmodern practices in early childhood teacher education', *Journal of Teacher Education*, 56(1): 34–45.

Siraj-Blatchford, J. and Siraj-Blatchford, I. (eds) (1995) *Educating the Whole Child: Cross Curricular Skills, Themes and Dimensions*. Buckingham: Open University Press.

Steinberg, S.R. and Kincheloe, J.L. (eds) (1998) *Kinderculture: The Corporate Construction of Childhood*. Boulder, CO: Westview Press.

Steiner, R. (1996) *The Education of the Child: and Early Lectures on Education*. New York: Anthroposophic Press.

Stephen, C., McPake, J., Plowman, L. and Berch-Heyman, S. (2008) 'Learning from the children: exploring preschool children's encounters with ICT at home', *Journal of Early Childhood Research*, 6(2): 99–117.

Suzuki, S. (2008) 'The effects of marital support, social network support, and parenting stress on parenting: self-efficacy among mothers of young children in Japan', *Journal of Early Childhood Research*, 8(1): 40–66.

Tobin, J., Hsueh, Y. and Karasawa M. (2009) *Preschool in Three Cultures Revisited: China, Japan, and the United States*. Chicago, IL: University of Chicago Press.

Tobin, J.J., Wu, D.Y.H. and Davidson, D.H. (1989) *Preschool in Three Cultures: Japan, China and the United States*. London: Yale University Press.

Welch, S. and Jones, P. (2010) *Rethinking Children's Rights: Attitudes in Contemporary Society*. London: Continuum.

Yelland, N. (ed.) (2005) *Critical Issues in Early Childhood Education*. Buckingham: Open University Press.

JOURNALS

In addition to Internet sources and books, international journals (many available online as well as in hard copy) are an important source of information on current research in early childhood education and care.

Childhood and Society
Childhoods Today
Early Child Development and Care
Early Childhood Matters
Early Education
Early Education and Development
Early Years
International Journal of Early Childhood Education
International Journal of Early Years Education
Journal of Early Childhood Literacy
Journal of Early Childhood Research

ORGANISATIONS

4 Nations Child Policy Network
4 Children (formerly Kids' Clubs Network)
Association Montessori Internationale
Alliance for Childhood
Bernard van Leer Foundation
Birth to Three Matters
British Association for Early Childhood Education
Bullying Online – helping parents and pupils deal with school bullying
capt – child accident prevention trust
Childcare Exchange
ChildLine
Community Playthings
Council for Awards in Children's Care and Education (CACHE)
Daycare Trust
Department for Education (DfE)
Early Childhood Australia Inc. (ECA)
Early Education
Early Learning Resource Unit (South Africa)
Educational Resources Information Centre – Clearing House for Elementary
    and Early Childhood Education (US)

For Parents by Parents
Foundation Stage
Learning Through Landscapes
National Association for the Education of the Young Child (NAEYC)
National Childminding Association (NCMA)
National Children's Bureau
National Day Nurseries Association (NDNA)
Northern Ireland Department of Education
NSPCC/EduCare Child Protection Awareness Programme
Nurture Group Network
Ofsted
OMEP (Organisation Mondiale pour l'Education Prescholaire)
Schools Out
Scottish Executive – Education Department (SEED) Learning and Teaching Scotland
Sightlines Initiative
Steiner Waldorf Fellowship
Talk to your baby – National Literacy Trust
The National Childbirth Trust
The Parenting Education and Support Forum
United Nations Educational, Scientific and Cultural Organisation (UNESCO)
Welsh Education Department
World Forum Foundation

INTERNET SOURCES

Due to the ever-changing nature of the World Wide Web, specific URL addresses are not included. However, most of the above organisations have useful websites which provide a range of information and useful links to other Internet sources.

978-1-84920-554-2   978-1-84920-578-8   978-1-4129-2309-5

978-1-84920-464-4   978-1-84920-196-4   978-1-84860-197-0

978-1-84920-116-2   978-1-84920-520-7   978-1-84860-997-6

Find out more about these titles and our wide range of books for education students and practitioners at **www.sagepub.co.uk/education**

EXCITING EARLY YEARS AND PRIMARY TEXTS FROM SAGE

978-1-84860-616-6   978-1-84920-030-1   978-1-84920-114-8

978-1-84860-713-2   978-1-84920-076-9   978-1-84920-126-1   978-1-84920-078-3

Find out more about these titles and our wide range
of books for education students and practitioners at
www.sagepub.co.uk/education

EXCITING EDUCATION TEXTS FROM SAGE

978-1-84920-464-4

978-1-4129-4674-2

978-1-4129-4498-4

978-1-4129-2913-4

978-1-4129-0814-6

Find out more about these titles and our wide range of books for education students and practitioners at **www.sagepub.co.uk/education**

ALSO FROM CATHY NUTBROWN